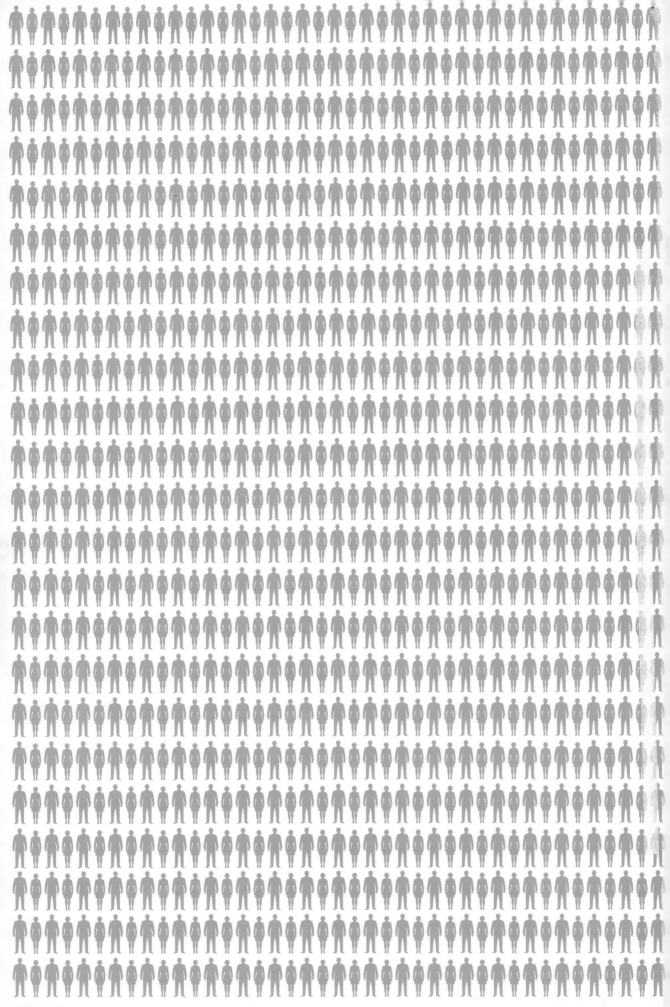

The
Filth

Rx

Special thanks to Steve Bunche,
Gary Erskine, David Drage and my
wife, Karen, for all their support
during the making of this book.
— **Chris Weston**

For Cheesy and Toby.
— **Grant Morrison**

Karen Berger Editor – Original Series   Steve Bunche Zachary Rau Assistant Editors – Original Series   Scott Nybakken Editor   Robbin Brosterman Design Director – Books   Shelly Bond Executive Editor – Vertigo
Hank Kanalz Senior VP – Vertigo & Integrated Publishing
Diane Nelson President   Dan DiDio and Jim Lee Co-Publishers   Geoff Johns Chief Creative Officer   Amit Desai Senior VP – Marketing & Franchise Management   Amy Genkins Senior VP – Business & Legal Affairs
Nairi Gardiner Senior VP – Finance   Jeff Boison VP – Publishing Planning   Mark Chiarello VP – Art Direction & Design   John Cunningham VP – Marketing   Terri Cunningham VP – Editorial Administration
Larry Ganem VP – Talent Relations & Services   Alison Gill Senior VP – Manufacturing & Operations   Jay Kogan VP – Business & Legal Affairs, Publishing   Jack Mahan VP – Business Affairs, Talent
Nick Napolitano VP – Manufacturing Administration   Sue Pohja VP – Book Sales   Fred Ruiz VP – Manufacturing Operations   Courtney Simmons Senior VP – Publicity   Bob Wayne Senior VP – Sales

Library of Congress Cataloging-in-Publication Data

Morrison, Grant.
  The Filth deluxe edition / Grant Morrison ; illustrated by Chris
Weston and Gary Erskine.
      pages cm
  ISBN 978-1-4012-5545-9 (hardback)
  1. Graphic novels. I. Erskine, Gary. II. Weston, Chris,
1969- III. Title.
  PN6728.F477M67 2015
  741.5'9411—dc23
                                          2015000601

SUSTAINABLE
FORESTRY
INITIATIVE

Certified Chain of Custody
Promoting Sustainable Forestry
www.sfiprogram.org
SFI-00507

This label only applies to the text section.

The Filth

THE DELUXE EDITION

Grant Morrison Writer   Chris Weston Penciller   Gary Erskine Inker
Matt Hollingsworth (#01-03) HI-FI (#04-13) Colorists   Clem Robins Letterer
Segura Inc. Cover Art and Original Series Covers
THE FILTH created by Grant Morrison and Chris Weston

PATIENT PRODUCT INFORMATION

The Filth™

COMIC BOOK ISSUES 01-13

Please read this introduction carefully before you start to use THE FILTH.
If you have any questions or are not sure about anything, ask your doctor, pharmacist or comic book dealer.

WHAT IS THE FILTH?

The Filth contains the active ingredient metaphor.

- The rectangular, multi-colored comic books marked "The Filth" contain 500mg of active visual and thematic metaphor per issue. Comic books also contain the inactive ingredients paper and ink.

Metaphor is one of a group of problem-solving medicines known as figures-of-speech which are normally used to treat literal thinking and other diseases. Metaphor combines two or more seemingly unrelated concepts in a way which stimulates lateral thought processes and creativity. Patients using The Filth are required to participate in the generation of significant content by "interpreting" text and images which have been deliberately loaded with multiple, overlapping meanings and scales.

The comic book issues come in collected editions of 13 and are to be consumed optically.

WHAT IS THE FILTH USED FOR?

This comic book is used to treat all manner of disorders including internet pornography addiction, grief, insomnia, "mid-life" crisis, schizophrenia, the ignorance of samsara and the 21st century blues, especially in patients whose millennial anxiety and general paranoia has not yet responded to normal treatments.

WHEN MUST THE FILTH NOT BE USED?

- If your doctor has advised you to avoid the use of metaphor.

- If you refuse to acknowledge the mocking laughter of the Abyss.

- If you cannot face the fact that your entire immediate environment is a seething battlefield of microscopic predators, prey and excreta and, simultaneously, a rich and complex metaphor.

- If, without understanding how it happened, you have found yourself in a dark room breastfeeding two elderly men you hardly know.

- If you are taking certain "dumb" antibiotics present in most media.

- If you are allergic to comic books or any of the ingredients they contain.

- If you take high-dose vitamin A supplements or have high levels of cholesterol or triglycerides (a fat-like substance) in your blood.

WHEN YOU SHOULD BE EXTRA CAREFUL WHEN USING THE FILTH

Make sure your doctor knows if:

- You or members of your family have a history of brutality and stupidity dating back to the pre-Cambrian oceans.

- You or members of your family really think anyone is listening when you talk the shite you talk.

- You regularly use drugs to desensitize yourself against the violent entertainment you consume.

- You have a history of vague depression, all-pervading guilt and a denial of personal mortality despite living in the pampered luxury of a privileged capitalist democracy.

- If you experience severe diarrhea, stop reading The Filth and contact your doctor immediately.

Your night vision may be affected by this medicine and ultraviolet light may become visible to you, so avoid sun-beds and "Insecocutor" bug-killing lamps, as the glare may lead to blindness.

Special note for blood donors:

You should not donate blood in smug imitation of Christ either during or for at least one month after reading The Filth.

MAY THE FILTH BE USED DURING PREGNANCY OR WHILE BREASTFEEDING?

The Filth must NOT be taken during pregnancy.

The Filth MUST be taken during pregnancy.

The Filth must NOT be taken during breastfeeding.

The Filth MUST be taken during breastfeeding.

Scientific opinion remains undecided.

The Filth

IMPORTANT

The Filth will damage an unborn baby only if inserted into the body. Female readers must strictly follow these instructions.

- You must not become pregnant while reading The Filth.

- If you are a woman of childbearing age you should have been using an effective method of contraception for at least one month prior to starting The Filth.

HOW SHOULD THE FILTH BE READ?

- Always read the comic books as your doctor tells you to. Your doctor will tell you when and how much to read and what to think.

- The comic books can be read either one at a time or all at once. Take them with a meal or with a glass of milk and some recreational drugs.

- Occasionally feelings of isolation and alienation may become worse during the first phase of treatment. Your symptoms should improve with further treatment.

- A course of treatment is generally dictated by reading and interpreting speed, after which you are likely to remain free of symptoms for a long time.

- Repeated courses of therapy are not normally needed but if your symptoms re-occur significantly then you or your doctor may decide on repeat doses of The Filth.

- If you read too many issues at once or someone else accidentally reads your copies of The Filth, contact your doctor, comic book dealer or nearest hospital straight away.

WHAT ARE THE POSSIBLE UNWANTED EFFECTS OF THE FILTH?

- Eye irritation

Your eyes may feel abused and slightly inflamed after exposure to The Filth. This may especially be a problem if you wear contact lenses or big horse blinkers. Ask your comic dealer to suggest some less visually demanding entertainment immediately.

- Aches and pains

Some people have muscle aches and pains and occasionally soreness of the tendons when they are reading this comic book. This may be more likely if you remain motionless in bizarre and awkward positions while reading.

- Hair changes

You may notice some changes to your hair (it will have grown very slightly) after reading The Filth for a while. This is usually only temporary and your hair should return to its normal length following a brief visit to your hairdresser or barber.

- Mood changes

Some people have experienced mood changes (depression or other symptoms of mental disorder followed by an elated, orgasmic release phase) while reading The Filth and in rare cases suicide and attempts of suicide have been thwarted and made to look ridiculous by use of this medicine.

HOW SHOULD THE FILTH BE STORED?

- Keep this medicine out of the reach and sight of all but the wisest of children.

- REMEMBER this medicine is for you. Only a right c**t would tell you anything else.

- Do not store your medicine above 451° Fahrenheit.

FURTHER INFORMATION

You can get more information about The Filth from your doctor, pharmacist or comic book dealer or from the website at www.crackcomicks.com.

DATE OF PREPARATION

March 2004

The
Filth

 VS

Contains
23 Pages

SO WHAT'S SO GOOD ABOUT JAMES BOND?

SO I'M LIKE THAT AND SHE'S LIKE THAT "IT'S LIKE THAT" THE TWO OF US ARE LIKE THAT.

HE SAYS, "WALTER, YOU'RE AHEAD OF YOUR TIME ALL RIGHT AND I ONLY HOPE THERE'S A JOB FOR YOU IN THE YEAR 2025 'CAUSE THERE'S FUCK ALL IN THIS FUCKING TIME ZONE. YOU'RE FIRED."

WELL, HE KNOWS HOW TO TREAT A LADY FOR A START. COME ON.

I DIDN'T EVEN KNOW YOUR MUM *HAD* ALZHEIMER'S UNTIL I SAW HER ON THE FRONT PAGE, COVERED IN THAT WOMAN'S BLOOD.

GAMBLING ALL NIGHT, KNOCKING HER ABOUT LIKE A RAG DOLL, USING HER AS A HUMAN SHIELD...VERY ROMANTIC!

"AT LEAST I'LL *SEE* THE YEAR 2025," I SAYS.

YOU'LL LIVE TO *105*, WALTER. WHY WORK?

SLADE.

DON'T FUCK WITH THE FILTH.

IT'S THIS *NEW* THING THEY'VE GOT: IT'S WAY BEYOND ALZHEIMER'S.

WHAT ARE *YOU* LOOKING AT?

TONY?

THEY'RE ALL *MAD* OUT THERE, AREN'T THEY?

YOU'RE LUCKY YOU DON'T HAVE TO GO TO WORK, SON.

MEET THE EIGHT-YEAR-OLDS WHO WRESTLE *RATS* FOR BREAKFAST IN THE SEWERS OF THE CAPITAL...

TONIGHT'S WORLD IN REACTION PROBES "THE LOST CHILDREN OF EL BASTARDE."

MAN-SIZE TISSUES

THOUSANDS DEAD...MOURNING CONTINUES ALL OVER...

ALLOW *EMPEROR OF SIAM* SPECIAL BLACK RICE TO ADD THAT SOMETHING EXTRA TO YOUR LOVE LIFE!

HFF

IF YOU'VE GOT ONE...

KITTY LITTER

ARE YOU WILLING TO EXPOSE YOURSELF, MR. PRES...

UDD?

THEY WANT YOU SLADE.

THE HAND NEVER LETS GO.

YOU MEET THE FUNNIEST BUGGERS, TONY.

YOU REALLY DO.

PORNOGRAPHY. IT'S GOT THAT MAN'S NAME ON IT: THE DIVORCE FROM *BEFORE* US.

"HEAR CAROLINE SCREAM AS MIKE SHOVES HIS ELEVEN-INCH DICK IN... HER DAD."

EX-POLICEMAN. HANDY WITH HIS FISTS.

TT

WHY DO WE KEEP *GETTING* THESE?

"WET ME FROM ABOVE" "SPLUNK IN MY PASTA" "ONE-MAN GANGBANG"

WHAT DO YOU THINK ABOUT ALL THAT, TONY, SON? HUMANS ARE *DAFT*, AREN'T THEY?

"WHITE MEN WITH BLACK DICKS... FUCKING YOUR WIFE"

IT'S NOT REALLY MY SORT OF THING, THIS.

REMEMBER YOU WERE ONLY *FIVE* WHEN WE FIRST MOVED IN HERE AFTER MUM DIED.

YOU *DON'T*, DO YOU?

21

YOU WANT TO KNOW WHAT KIDNEY FAILURE'S LIKE?

ALL I HAVE TO DO IS PUSH.

YOU'LL FEEL A LITTLE SLEEPY, THAT'S ALL. YOU'LL JUST WANT TO LIE DOWN.

IT'S OKAY ...NOBODY'S GONNA TOUCH THE FUCKING CAT.

JESUS, SLADE! WE THOUGHT WE WERE DOING THE SCRAWNY BASTARD A FAVOR.

STOP CALLING ME "SLADE"...

IT DOESN'T EVEN KNOW YOU.

LOOK AT HIM; JUST BONES AND A SMELL.

ALL HE CARES ABOUT'S HIS NEXT CAN OF KITTY KRAP...

YOU DON'T WANT TO GET TOO CLOSE TO GREG'S THINGS, SLADE...

HE DOES KNOW ME.

TONY?

HE DOES KNOW ME.

THERE'S NOTHING WRONG WITH HIS KIDNEYS, I'VE BEEN FEEDING HIM HIS SPECIAL HOMEOPATHIC DIET...

COME ON, TONY.

HERE.

IT'S TURKEY HAM ON THE MENU TONIGHT.

SEE?

I'M GREGORY FEELY NOW.

TONY'S MY CAT.

DON'T LOOK SO GLUM.

COME ON. PUT THAT ON.

FIBERS IN THE TOUPÉE WILL SHIELD YOU FROM ELECTROMAGNETIC ATTACK.

OKAY.

TWO DROPS IN EACH EYE. THEY'LL HELP TO PROTECT YOUR EYEBALLS FROM COMPRESSION.

I'LL DRIVE.

GREG'S *NOT* A PERVERT. HE HAS HIS OWN TASTES, THAT'S ALL.

THERE'S NOTHING *WRONG* WITH HIM.

WHAT'S COMPRESSION AGAIN?

WHY DO I FEEL LIKE A FUCK-ING *COAT* SOMEONE'S BEEN WEARING OUT IN THE RAIN?

NICELY PUT. YOU SHOULD WRITE SONGS FOR INDIE BANDS.

"THE HAND NEVER LETS GO," SLADE. YOU KNOW THAT. YOU'RE BACK ON ACTIVE DUTY NOW...

PEOPLE KEEP TELLING ME.

AAOOWM?

The Filth

VENEREAL **ARTS**, OR SOFT INDUSTRIES, ARE BASED IN **THE FINGER**, UNDER CHIEF CONSTABLE **BABALON MANDRILL**.

HERE, DESIRE AND SHAME ARE EXPLORED AND POLICED BY THE PLANET'S VICE SQUAD.

THE HORNS, OF COURSE, DEAL WITH THE DEEPEST, MOST **NEGATIVE** CORNERS OF THE HUMAN EXPERIENCE...MURDER, HATRED, DARKNESS, FEAR AND ALIENATION.

BUT YOU'LL MEET THE **SCIENCE GESTAPO** SOON ENOUGH...

BOLLOCKS.

WHO ARE YOU?

THIS IS THE VOICE OF **MOTHER DIRT**, YOUR SUPERIOR OFFICER.

OFFICER SPARTACUS HUGHES HAS SET IN MOTION A NUMBER OF THREATS TO **SOCIAL HYGIENE**.

THAT'S WHY WE'RE ASSIGNING A NEW ELITE TEAM, UNDER **YOUR** COMMAND, SLADE.

OURS **IS** THE HAND THAT WIPES THE ARSE OF THE WORLD, REMEMBER?

THIS IS A JOKE.

THIS IS A FUCKING JOKE.

WHEN DO I WAKE UP AND SMEAR MY PADDED CELL WITH MY OWN FECES?

I WISH YOU'D STOP BEING SO GODDAMN *WEIRD.*

IT'S BAD FOR *MORALE,* SOME OF THESE PEOPLE WE'RE WORKING WITH CAN BE VERY HIGHLY STRUNG.

ALERT!

OFFICERS SLADE AND SPECTOR!

SLADE AND SPECTOR REPORT TO MAN GREEN/MAN YELLOW.

MAKING SURE THEY'RE ASLEEP WHILE WE OPERATE...

"SLADE"? ISN'T THAT SUPPOSED TO BE ME?

IGNORE IT.

TIME MEANS NOTHING TO MAN GREEN/MAN YELLOW AND YOU HAVEN'T EVEN *MET* CAMERON SPECTOR YET SO I WOULDN'T WORRY TOO MUCH.

FINGER ALERT: ROGUE BIO-ENGINEERED ANTI-PERSON TARGETED.

LOOK, YOU DON'T SEEM LIKE A BAD PERSON. YOU SEEM VERY... *DEDICATED,* OFFICER NIL.

BUT I WOKE UP AS SOMEONE *DIFFERENT* THIS MORNING...

FOR THE MILLIONTH TIME, SINCE WE *STARTED,* YOUR NAME IS EDWARD SLADE, SPECIAL OFFICER 999 OF *THE HAND.* I DON'T CARE *WHO* YOU GOT OUT OF BED AS.

AND MY NAME IS *MIAMI,* OKAY?

WE'RE *GARBAGEMEN,* NED.

WE STOP THE WORLD'S BACK YARD FROM *STINKING.*

HOW HARD IS THAT TO UNDER-STAND?

I'M BEGINNING TO DESPISE YOU.

CLEANING UP THE SHIT BEFORE THEY SEE IT

GET ME INTELLIGENCE!!

WE'RE CONTAINING OFFICER HUGHES AS BEST WE CAN BUT WE NEED EXPERT HELP FROM *THE PALM*.

JESUS...

THESE I-LIFE CREATURES...

THEY GOT *LOOSE* AND DID SOMETHING TO A BUNCH OF *NUDE* SWINGERS INSIDE.

BY THE LOOKS OF THINGS THEY FOUND OUT HOW TO TAKE CONTROL OF BASIC HUMAN FUNCTIONS AND MAKE 'EM THEIR OWN.

WE'RE PICKING THEM OFF FROM HERE IN CASE THEY GET CLOSE ENOUGH TO *IDIOTIZE* ANY MORE OF OUR OWN PEOPLE.

IDIOTIZE?

SHIT.

LOOK, LEAVE THE CLEAN-UP TO US.

CLEAN-UP?

WHERE DO WE START?

FREQUENCY NEGOTIATORS WENT IN THERE TO TALK SPARTACUS HUGHES DOWN, SIR.

THEY ALL CAME OUT ACTING LIKE RETARDED *CHILDREN*: SHITTING THEMSELVES, SPOUTING GIBBERISH AND GENERALLY LETTING THE SIDE DOWN.

WE'RE LEADING THEM INTO THE QUARANTINE TENT BY PLAYING EARLY '90s *TECHNO*.

THEY FOLLOW THAT OLD SKOOL BEAT LIKE DRUGGED RATS CHASING THE PIED PIPER.

MY BACKUP IS *YOU* AND A TALKING CHIMPANZEE WITH A SNIPER RIFLE, AM I RIGHT?

COMRADE 9, THE WORLD'S *GREATEST* ASSASSIN, YOU RADIOACTIVE LUMP OF TURD.

AND I HAVE TO *TALK* TO SOMEONE CALLED *SPARTACUS HUGHES* BECAUSE HE KILLED SOMEONE *ELSE*?...

:KK: YOU'RE *RIGHT* ABOUT SLADE WAKING UP A TOTAL ASSHOLE.

I'D RATHER HAVE *DAS KAPITAL* SHOVED UP MY ASS WITH A *STICK* THAN CALL THAT PIECE OF IMPERIALIST SHIT MY FRIEND!

SHIT CHIMP!

HRR HURRN

SHIT CHIMP, KILL! KILL! KILL FOR KHRUSHCHEV!

PHOORT

THE UNEXPECTED ELEMENT WHICH UNDERMINED HUGHES' *POISE* AND ALLOWED US TO *STRIKE*.

YOU PLAYED YOUR PART *PERFECTLY*. YOU MUST SEE THAT NOW.

BUT WHAT DID HE *MEAN*?

HE SAID "ANYONE CAN BE SPARTACUS HUGHES"?

SOMETIMES IGNORANCE *IS* BLISS, SPECIAL CONSTABLE SLADE.

OFFICER HUGHES WAS *INSANE*, A HIGHLY TRAINED DESTROYER FROM *THE FIST*.

BUT YOUR *AMNESIA* MADE YOU JUST STUPID ENOUGH TO *FORGET* HOW DANGEROUS HE WAS.

HE WAS EXPECTING A FULLY ACTIVE NED SLADE, NOT A SEMI-AMNESIAC...

THERE'S SOMETHING YOU'RE NOT TELLING.

THAT'S *ALWAYS* TRUE BUT YOU'RE TOLD AS MUCH AS YOU *NEED* TO PERFORM EACH OF YOUR DUTIES AS A SANITATION OFFICER OF *THE HAND*.

SOCIAL HYGIENE DEPENDS ON YOU AND PEOPLE LIKE YOU.

YOU *KNEW* THAT WHEN YOU JOINED.

BUT I CAN'T REMEMBER WHO I WAS WHEN I *STARTED*?

The
Filth

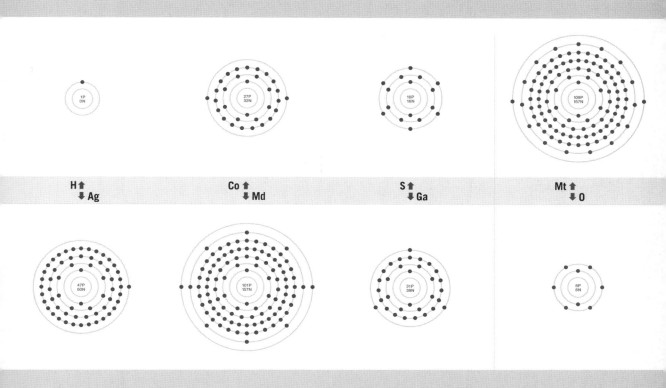

H ⬆ ⬇ Ag   Co ⬆ ⬇ Md   S ⬆ ⬇ Ga   Mt ⬆ ⬇ O

03.STRUCTURES AND ULTRASTRUCTURES   22 PAGES

WITHOUT WARNING!!!

MY AUNT RUNS THE FLOWER SHOP. *THAT'S* SORT OF PSYCHEDELIC, ISN'T IT?

FLOWERS AND SHIT.

AH, I WISH SOMETHING GREAT WOULD HAPPEN.

STONER CUNTS!

BUT NOT AS PSYCHEDELIC AS THE FACT THAT THE PLANET EARTH HAS ITS OWN *RING*.

WHAT? LIKE A TELEPHONE?

NO, LIKE *SATURN*.

A RING OF ORBITING, ANIMAL ASTRONAUTS, ALL DEAD.

WANKERS!

HEY, THAT'S *ENOUGH!*

DON'T LOOK AT THAT MAN, LAURIE, LOVE. HE'S NOT NICE.

THERE'S THAT STRAY KITTEN WE'VE BEEN FEEDING, LITTLE *BARNEY*.

I SHOULD TAKE HIM *IN*, SHOULDN'T I?

YOU WOULDN'T MIND, WOULD YOU, TONY?

MMM, YOUR FANNY LOOKS PRETTY TASTY TO ME, MISS.

BRRRT BRRRT

GOOD BOY. YOU'RE A GOOD BOY, TONY.

SHH.

DON'T WORRY.

HE'S VERY PATIENT WITH THESE BLOOD TESTS.

I WISH THEY WERE *ALL* LIKE HIM, MR. FEELY.

I KNOW.

I'VE ALWAYS SAID HE EXPECTED TO GROW UP INTO A HUMAN BEING.

FELINE HIV

I THINK HE WAS ALWAYS QUITE SURPRISED HE STAYED A CAT.

THEY BECOME LIKE *FAMILY,* DON'T THEY?

BREAKS YOUR HEART.

AH NO.

F893 FIN

TONY'S LOST WEIGHT AGAIN AND IT'S *YOUR* FAULT; FEEDING HIM THAT CRAP FROM TINS, JUST TO SAVE *MONEY*...

I DON'T *NEED* A STAND-IN OR A STUNT DOUBLE OR WHATEVER YOU ARE ANYMORE; I'VE *RESIGNED* FROM THE HAND.

YOU CAN BE "SPECIAL OFFICER NED SLADE" IF YOU WANT.

THERE'S A VACANCY.

MMRRFF

ALL RIGHT!

BZZT BZZT

THIS ONE COULDN'T BE MORE THAN TEN YEARS OLD.

THEY TRAP THEM IN INTERNET ROOMS WITH PROMISES OF CHEATS FROM VIDEO GAMES. THERE WAS A CRIMEWATCH ALL ABOUT IT.

SOMEBODY SHOULD BE PHONING THE POLICE.

PHWEEZE

FLOOD INK CHAMBER.

CONTINUITY ONLINE.

RUN.

INVISIBLE FROM HERE...YET SEEMING TO PASS THRU US AND INTO OUR FUTURE.

HOW CAN WE AVENGE OUR COMRADES WHEN THE THREAT IS AN UNSEEN ONE, TRAVELLING THRU TIME?

REWIND.

STOP.

RUN CONTINUITY.

...YET TO PASS AND INTO FUTURE.

HOW CAN WE AVENGE OUR COMRADES WHEN THE THREAT IS UNSEEN TRAVELLING TI...

MY WHOLE LIFE'S FALLING APART, ADAM!

DON'T GO! PLEASE DON'T GO INTO THIS STUPID "OVERSPHERE" YOU'VE DISCOVERED!

S.O.

S.O.

BUT IF THE OVERSPHERE BARRIER TRULY EXISTS ONLY MY CRYPTO-CONSCIOUS-NESS CAN PIERCE IT!

SOMETHING FROM BEYOND THAT VEIL IS TAMPERING WITH OUR VERY LIVES, EVE! ONLY I IN MY GUISE AS SECRET ORIGINAL CAN HOPE TO CONTACT AND BARGAIN WITH THE MONSTROUS UN-TELLIGENCES WHICH DWELL THERE!

THIS COULD BE MY CHANCE TO PREVENT THE ULTIMATE CRIME, THE COSMIC CRIME, AND RESTORE FREE WILL TO THE UNIVERSE.

AND WHY? SO THAT MORE PEOPLE WILL LOVE YOU? THE WHOLE EARTH ALREADY LOVES YOU! THEY EVEN LOVE YOU ON OTHER PLANETS!

NOW YOU WANT THE ADORATION OF ALL CREATION!

ISN'T THE LOVE OF ONE GOOD WOMAN ENOUGH FOR YOU, ADAM?

EVE! STOP!... PLEASE... IT'S NOT WHAT YOU THINK...

EVE! STOP!... PLEASE... IT'S NOT WHAT YOU THINK...

NE MAN FOR DAM?

STOP.

OH, EVE. IF ONLY I COULD SEE YOU. IF ONLY I COULD TALK TO YOU AGAIN BUT I FLEW TOO HIGH AND BROKE AGAINST THE WALLS OF HEAVEN, EVE. YOU WERE RIGHT.

I SEE THE CRUEL REALITY BEHIND ALL OUR HOPES AND DREAMS NOW. I KNOW US FOR WHAT WE TRULY ARE.

NOT SUPERMEN BUT SUPER-SLAVES IN A SYNTHETIC PRISON.

PLAYING OUT CRUMMY MEANINGLESS ADVENTURES WRITTEN BY AMORAL MONSTERS.

THEY FARM US, EVE; THEY FARM US FOR THE WONDERS WE SIMPLY ACCEPT IN OUR IGNORANCE.

THERE ARE EVEN PORNOGRAPHIC VERSIONS OF OUR LIVES, MY LOVE.

ALTERNATIVE CONTINUITIES WHERE YOU LET THE ENTIRE STATUS QUORUM GANGBANG YOU FOR MONEY TO PAY YOUR RENT.

SICK SEX SITUATIONS I'D NEVER EVEN THOUGHT OF UNTIL I FOUND MERCURY'S FILES...THE SIDEWAYS LIVES HE'D WRITTEN FOR US TO LIVE...

I PULL OUT AND RUN THOSE ROTTEN STORIES EVERY NIGHT, EVE. I CAN'T HELP IT.

I...I LOVE TO WATCH YOU LOSE YOUR COOL AND YOUR DECENCY EVERY NIGHT BECAUSE IT'S THE CLOSEST I CAN GET...TO HOW IT ONCE FELT TO LOVE YOU.

MAN-RO HELP ME. I KEEP THINKING I'LL FIND A WAY TO SAVE US ALL.

THEN I JUST WASTE ANOTHER FIVE HOURS CHECKING OUT SLEAZY HARDCORE COMIX.

The
Filth

22 Pages

YOU'VE *ALREADY* GOT THEM ALL *TALKING* ABOUT ME ROUND HERE!

I SPENT *AGES* BUILDING UP GREG'S LIFE AND NOW YOU'RE JUST FUCKING IT UP!

LOOK AT *TONY!*

LOOK AT THE *STATE* OF HIM! HE'S HALF *DEAD.*

THAT'S BETTER THAN THE THREE QUARTERS DEAD HE WAS YESTER-DAY, IF YOU ASK ME.

NO, THERE'S SOMETHING *WRONG* WITH ALL THIS.

IT'S ALL RIGHT, TONY... I'LL BE BACK SOON WITH SOMETHING NICE FOR YOUR TEA, SON...

JUST DO THIS *ONE* FUCKING THING *RIGHT,* WILL YOU?

I DON'T CARE *WHAT* YOU DO TO GREG. WILL YOU PLEASE JUST TAKE CARE OF TONY?

HE'S GOT BLOOD TEST RESULTS TO GET...

WELL, MAYBE IF YOU DON'T GO *NUTS* AND TIE ME UP IN THE CUPBOARD AGAIN, I'LL BE ABLE TO READ HIM A FUCKING BEDTIME *STORY* IN MEOW-MEOW LANGUAGE, SLADE.

MAYBE I'LL READ HIM *"NOT MY ARSE, INSPECTOR!"* FROM THE COLLECTION UNDER THE BED.

HORT.

THAT SOUNDS LIKE SHIT.

NO MORE TALK FOR YOU, SLADE.

DUTY CALLS.

82

DOCTOR *ARNO VON VERMUN* ?

I'M NED SLADE; PALM LIAISON.

AH-AH!

IN THE *EAST*, THE LEFT HAND IS USED TO WIPE ONE'S *ANUS* AFTER DEFECATION.

LET ME GUESS...

SNNFF

YOU'VE BEEN ATTENDING TO A *CAT*...A NEUTERED *TOM* WITH A *THYROID* COMPLAINT.

YOU RECENTLY DUG A SMALL *GRAVE* FOR ANOTHER ANIMAL.

THYROID?

IS THIS *TELEPATHY?*

OR DID YOU READ MY *DOSSIER?*

NOT AT ALL.

EVERY MAN AND WOMAN HAS A UNIQUE, PERSONAL *CLOUD*, OFFICER SLADE.

THIS SEETHING AURA OF INVISIBLE PARTICLES FOLLOWS EACH OF US EVERY-WHERE WE GO.

THE CARPENTER HAMMERS OUT A NEBULA OF WOOD SHAVINGS AND SWEAT; THE TEACHER WEARS AN INVISIBLE GOWN OF CHALK DUST; THE SECRET *FETISHIST* HIDES PARTICLES OF RUBBER AND SILICONE SPRAY BEHIND HER TWEED FRAGMENTS.

THE CLOUD NEVER LIES.

WHICH IS WHY I CAN CONFIDENTLY SAY THAT OUR POOR VICTIM HERE WAS *MURDERED*...

HE SMELLS OF THE *DRAINS*, WHERE THE SLIME OF THE UNIVERSE DRIBBLES DOWN INTO DARKNESS.

SHALL WE VISIT?

...SOMETIMES A WORKER WILL JUST GO BUGFUCK AND SKIN-EYED WHAT WITH ALL THE TITS AND COCKS, AND THEY TRY TO CLIMB TOWARDS THE *PEAKS*, LOOKING FOR *HARDER* STUFF, THINGS THEY HAVEN'T SEEN OR EVEN IMAGINED.

THEY JUST KEEP CLIMBING IN A FEVER AND USUALLY DIE UP THERE WHEN THEIR SUITS WEAR OUT; TIME MOVES EVEN *FASTER* AT HIGHER ALTITUDES.

SO "MORALE" IS A WORD WE REFUSE TO EVEN ACKNOWLEDGE OR RECOGNIZE OUT HERE AT *LANDFILL STATION XXX.*

BIOLOGICAL WASTE, STICKY USED PORN AND DEAD JUNKIES WHO GOT FLUSHED BY MISTAKE; THIS'D BE A WONDERFUL LIFE IF I HADN'T GROWN UP DREAMING OF A JOB AS A GLAMOR PHOTOGRAPHER.

05. Pornomancer

22 PAGES

THERE IS NOTHING MORE I CAN SAY.

HOW ABOUT THE STORY OF *YOU*; YOU'RE A VERY SEXY LADY, THAT'S FROM WHERE I'M SITTING.

JONES, JENESIS

WANTED
WILFRED ROBBERY
NICOLA MARI

MISSING
ADELA STEELE

WAN
ON MURDER
CHRISTIA

WELL.. I KNOW YOU CAME OUT OF *NOWHERE* FIVE YEARS AGO.

I KNOW YOU HAVE A NOVELTY PENIS WHICH DEFIES MEDICAL ANALYSIS.

OTHERWISE *DON'T* TRY TO FUCK WITH ME, ANDERS; I HAVE *PMS*.

SPERM SPECIMEN.

PLEASE.

SURE.

THIS IS WHAT I DO FOR A LIVING.

JESUS.

The Filth™

#06
THE WORLD OF
ANDERS KLIMAKKS

I'M NOT SURE *WHAT* THE LITTLE ONES EAT.

I PUT SOME OF THAT ROTTEN OLD MICROWAVE *CHILI* IN THERE FOR THEM AND IT SEEMS TO HAVE DONE THE TRICK.

SEE THE LITTLE *CITIES*... THEY LOOK LIKE *MOLD* SPORES BUT THEY LIGHT UP AT NIGHT.

I-LIFE THEY CALL IT.

I SHOULDN'T BE KEEPING *ANY* OF THIS STUFF, SHOULD I?

IT'S NOT EVEN SUPPOSED TO *EXIST,* WHATEVER THAT'S SUPPOSED TO MEAN.

I COULDN'T JUST LET THE POOR, TINY LITTLE THINGS *DIE,* COULD I?

I'LL SIT THEM DOWN HERE WHERE THEY CAN SEE THE TELLY IF THEY LIKE.

I'M GOING TO DO SOMETHING I'VE NEVER DONE BEFORE, BABY...

I'M GOING TO MILK A VENOMOUS SPIDER FOR KICKS!

AND HIM.

"ANDERS KLIMAKKS".

HE'S NOT SUPPOSED TO EXIST EITHER...AND I'M...I'M NOT SUPPOSED TO *HAVE* HORRIBLE STUFF LIKE THIS AROUND THE HOUSE...BUT MAX WANTED PROOF...

MMMMM DO IT TO MEEEE!

IT'S THAT OTHER MAN, ISN'T IT?

HAS HE BEEN *DRINKING,* TONY?

143

COME ON, TONY, YOU'RE MY BEST PAL.

YOU'RE ALL I'VE GOT.

PLEASE DON'T LET ANYTHING HAPPEN TO YOU.

OH MUM, PLEASE DON'T LET ANYTHING HAPPEN TO HIM.

I WOULDN'T *KNOW* IF I'D GONE MAD. YOU *DON'T*, DO YOU?

WHAT IF I'VE *ALWAYS* BEEN MAD AND NOW THEY'RE ALL JUST FINDING OUT?

SHIT!

HANG ON, SON. I WON'T LET THEM HURT YOU.

HULLO, OFFICER?

IS SOMETHING *WRONG?*

I'M JUST ABOUT TO PHONE THE EMERGENCY *VET:* MY CAT'S LEGS WENT A BIT FUNNY...

I'M A BIT WORRIED...

YOU *SHOULD* BE, SUN-SHINE.

GREGORY JOHN FEELY: THIS IS A SEARCH WARRANT FOR THESE PREMISES.

SEARCH WARRANT

147

GOODBYE, FREAKSHOW.

PASSPORT
RABIES

WHY GO OFF-BOAT, WHEN YOU CAN GET ALL THE ACTION YOU NEED RIGHT *HERE,* YOU FRIGID BITCH!

I'D RATHER LIVE IN *AUSTRALIA;* I LIKED IT WHEN WE WERE *THERE.*

UP *YOURS,* RUDI.

DON'T THESE PEOPLE REALIZE THEY'RE LIVING ON THE EIGHTH WONDER OF THE WORLD?

WHY'S EVERYBODY SO UPTIGHT?

YOU COULD RUN FOR *WEEKS* AND NEVER HIT THE EDGE.

DON'T LOOK AT *ME...*

WHAT'S UP *NOW?*

LOWER DECK ASSHOLES COMPLAINING ABOUT BEING *SHAT* ON AGAIN; AT LEAST THEY'RE NEAR THE FUCKING *LIFE-BOATS!*

LIBERTY EQUALITY FRATERNITY NOT LIKELY!

FIX MY FRIDGE

FUCK OFF!

HELL NO!

DRINKING WATER NOT SALT WATER!

YOUR DAD'S THE *CAPTAIN!* CAN'T YOU FORCE HIM TO MAKE LIFE *PERFECT* FOR EVERYONE?

I MEAN, THE WAY IT'S *MEANT* TO BE?

SHIT, I'M THE FUCKING PRESIDENT.

≈PHEWW≈

NAME'S NEVILLE QUAIN... HEAD OF SECURITY.

I DON'T REMEMBER MEETING YOU AT THE BRIEFING EARLIER...

LET'S HOPE IT'S NOT ALZHEIMER'S MISTER QUAIN.

THINK OF ME AS A TAROT CARD: I REPRESENT "OPPORTUNITIES ABOUT TO ARISE."

MORPHINE.

THEY DID SOME VERY INTERESTING AND DOWNRIGHT INHUMANE EXPERIMENTS WITH RAT COLONIES, NEVILLE.

A GREAT LEAP FOR MANKIND.

THEY FOUND WHEN CERTAIN POPULATION LIMITS ARE REACHED, ALL IT TAKES IS THE ADDITION OF ONE EXTRA RAT...

AND THE WHOLE COMMUNITY SLIDES INTO UNSTOPPABLE CHAOS.

WHAT?

FUCK ARE YOU SELLING?

HELP ME WITH THIS SACK OF SHIT!

ONE LITTLE RAT AND UTOPIA TURNS INTO RWANDA.

FASCINATING.

FASCINATING STUFF, MISTER...

WHAT IS YOUR NAME?

I'M THE PRESIDENT...

I'M A POWERFUL MAN...

PLEASE DON'T...I HATE NEEDLES...I HAVE MONEY IN MY JACKET...

FIRST HIT'S ALWAYS *FREE*, SIR.

NAAAUU

MONEY MEANS *NOTHING*; *ART* IS OUR GOD.

WE'RE GIVING THE PRESIDENT *BREASTS*, MISTER QUAIN. WHETHER HE LIKES IT OR NOT.

MAGNIFICENT BREASTS! BIGGER THAN THE SUN!

AUUU

EVER SINCE I WAS A POWERLESS LITTLE BOY I'VE HAD A *DREAM*.

I'VE WANTED TO FUCK THE PRESIDENT IN THE ASS WHILE HE SINGS "HAPPY BIRTHDAY," JUST LIKE *MARILYN MONROE*.

MAKE IT SO.

I'M AN EXPERT IN SOCIAL EROSION TECHNIQUES, MARTIAL ARTS AS APPLIED TO WHOLE *SOCIETIES;* TAMING AND BREAKING A CULTURE IS THE SAME AS BRAINWASHING A HUMAN BEING.

BUT IT'S WHAT HAPPENS *AFTER* THAT INTERESTS ME.

I'M SICK OF SIN, SPARTACUS.

GOOD.

I'VE SPENT THE LAST FEW DAYS FULFILLING EVERY SICK AND TWISTED *FANTASY* THAT EVER CRAWLED AROUND IN BACK OF MY HEAD.

ALL BUT ONE.

THE CITIZENS OF LIBERTANIA ARE IN A SOFT, RAW, PLIABLE STATE OF *SHOCK,* NEVILLE.

READY TO IMPRINT *NEW* RULES AND A NEW PURPOSE.

WHAT *ARE* YOU?

WHO THE HELL ARE YOU *WORKING* FOR, SPARTACUS?

I DON'T *WORK,* NEVILLE. I *PLAY.*

THE LIBERTANIA IS LIKE A LITTLE *MODEL* OF THE WORLD...

I LIKE TOYS.

I LIKE *YOU,* SPARTACUS.

YOU'VE BROUGHT A WELCOME RAY OF SUNSHINE INTO THIS SADISTIC OLD FOOL'S DULL JOURNEY TOWARDS THE *RETIREMENT* HOME.

I COULD LISTEN TO YOU TALK ALL DAY.

BROTHERS AND SISTERS!

THE REIGN OF RED CHAOS IS OVER! THE CORRUPT POWER ELITES OF THE LIBERTANIA HAVE BEEN OVERTHROWN!

...GOT ALL THAT? WHEN SOCIAL BONDS DISINTEGRATE, THE WORST THINGS YOU CAN *IMAGINE* START TO HAPPEN ON A DAILY BASIS.

PEOPLE HAVE DEGENERATED INTO FRENZIED PIRATE BLOOD-LUST...

EXPECT CANNIBAL BEHAVIOR, INCEST, FRATRICIDE, SELF-MUTILATION AND PET MICROWAVING...

BE READY FOR

ANY-THING.

BUDDY, CAN YOU SPARE A DIME BAG?

GO ON THEN.

LET'S SEE YOU DO YOUR *DANCE* AGAIN, MR. PRESIDENT.

DO YOUR *SEXY DANCE* FOR WORLD PEACE.

THAT'S IT! I *PAID* FOR THOSE PRIZE-WINNING PROSTHETICS AND I WANT TO *SEE* THEM IN ACTION.

♪ PRIVATE DANCERR ♪

...FUCK ME... HELP ME...

SMACK ME UP.

HELLO, NED.

THAT'S THE GREAT THING ABOUT DEMOCRACY: *ANY-ONE* CAN BE PRESIDENT.

AND THE PRESIDENT CAN BE *ANY-ONE.*

SMACK ME UP

ME FUKKEE SUKKEE! FIVE DORRA!

190

...SO-CALLED EIGHTH WONDER OF THE WORLD SINKS TITS UP IN SEA... HORROR AS SHARKS DEVOUR THE LIVING AND THE DEAD WITH THE SAME INDISCRIMINATE ZEAL...

SHIP SINKS

THAT'S GOT ME *THINKING*, THAT HAS; I'VE ALWAYS *FANCIED* A CARIBBEAN CRUISE.

SEE, IF IT WASN'T FOR *YOU*, CAT, I COULD GO ON A DECENT *HOLIDAY*.

COME ON, *WORK* FOR IT!

I WOULDN'T HAVE ANY FUCKING *RESPONSIBILITIES*, WOULD I? I WOULDN'T BE SO STRESSED OUT AND MAD.

IF IT WASN'T FOR *YOUR* STUPID, UGLY FACE.

TOO LATE!

MMM

NYUM NYUM

DID I FORGET TO GIVE YOU *THESE*, TONY?

NYUM NYUM

NYUM NYUM NYUM

The Filth

09

PROJECT TITLE **INSIDE THE HAND**

PRIMARY ARCHITECTS GRANT MORRISON   CHRIS WESTON GARY ERSKINE

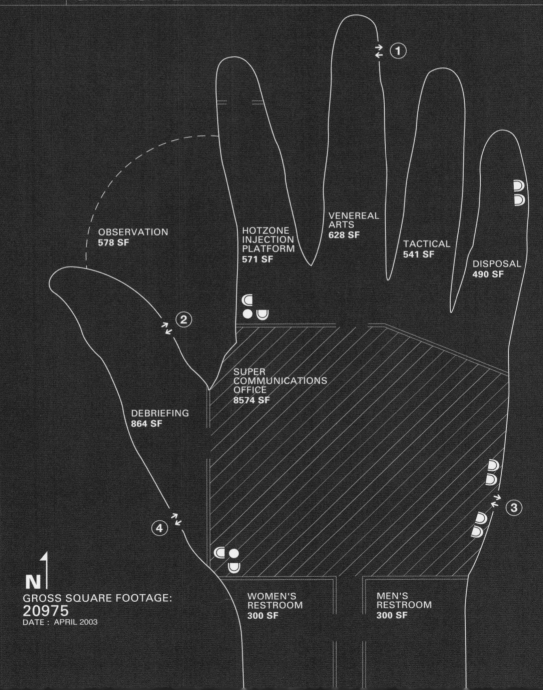

OBSERVATION
578 SF

HOTZONE
INJECTION
PLATFORM
571 SF

VENEREAL
ARTS
628 SF

TACTICAL
541 SF

DISPOSAL
490 SF

SUPER
COMMUNICATIONS
OFFICE
8574 SF

DEBRIEFING
864 SF

N

GROSS SQUARE FOOTAGE:
20975
DATE : APRIL 2003

WOMEN'S
RESTROOM
300 SF

MEN'S
RESTROOM
300 SF

YOU! WHY DIDN'T I GET TO SEE HIM?

WHERE'S HIS BODY!

I'M SORRY?

WHY DIDN'T I GET TO SAY GOODBYE?

BUT YOU DID...

YOU BROUGHT HIM IN YOURSELF, TWO... TWO DAYS AGO?...

THAT WASN'T ME! THAT WAS MY EVIL LOOK-ALIKE!

WHERE'S TONY'S BODY!

...WE...WE SENT IT OUT IN THE VAN WITH A BATCH FOR THE VET SCHOOL...THE STUDENTS... FOR...FOR DISSECTION.

YOU WERE QUITE SURE YOU DIDN'T WANT THE BOTHER OF HOME BURIAL...

DISSECTION, IS IT!

PUT THAT DOWN, MISTER FEELY. WITHOUT THAT MEDICINE A PAIR OF GOLDEN HAMSTERS MIGHT NOT LAST THE NIGHT...

DON'T BOTHER THE POLICE.

I OUTRANK THEM!

CALL ME A FUCKING TAXI!!

PETS ARE FUNNY AREN'T THEY?

MATE OF MINE FROM SCHOOL USED TO HAVE A TARANTULA SPIDER THAT DID AN IMPRESSION OF WINSTON CHURCHILL IF YOU POKED ITS FACE WITH A PENCIL...

CAN YOU WAIT FOR ME, DRIVER?

I WON'T BE LONG.

I WANT MY FUCKING CAT BACK!!!

I WANT TONY AND I DON'T WANT HIM IN BITS!!!

IT'S ALL RIGHT, TONY

THEY WON'T GET YOU.

...AND THEN TRY BURYING A HORSE IN A SHOEBOX IN THE BACK GARDEN. YOU WON'T GET FAR BEFORE SELF-DOUBT STARTS CREEPING IN.

AM I BEING DISCIPLINED?

WHAT *IS* THIS, SPECTOR?

WHAT HAVE YOU *DONE* TO GREG'S LIFE?

EEZ LIFE WISNY REAL! IT WIS AW *MADE UP*, FUR FUKK'S SAKE! MENNY TIMES JIHUVTY BE TELT?

AN NOO WUR SHUTTEN IT *DOON* TAY STOAP YOO FAY LOSING THE FUKKEN HEED AWTHEGITHER.

ALERT! OFFICERS SLADE AND SPECTOR!

SLADE AND SPECTOR REPORT TO MAN GREEN/ MAN YELLOW.

MAN GREEN/ MAN YELLOW?

WHERE DID I HEAR THAT BEFORE?

"TIME MEANS NOTHING TO MAN GREEN/ MAN YELLOW."

YIR RIGHT THERR.

CHIEF CONSTABLES IH THE PALM.

RIGHT, YOU.

IN.

THE SCIENCE GESTAPO'S HAD FUKKEN ENUFFY YOO AN YIR SHITE.

COME.

205

I'D LIKE A NICE CHEERFUL-LOOKING BOUQUET

I'M NOT SURE...

IS IT FOR SOMEONE SPECIAL?

WELL... IT'S FOR MY CAT, ACTUALLY.

HE JUST PASSED AWAY AND... AND I WANTED SOMETHING TO PUT IN HIS PAWS.

HE WAS MY BEST FRIEND FOR FIFTEEN YEARS.

I MISS HIM SO MUCH ALREADY...

I KEEP LOOKING AT THE TINS OF FOOD LEFT OVER...I KEEP EXPECTING TO SEE HIM POPPING HIS HEAD ROUND THE DOOR...

WHO'S GOING TO WAKE ME UP AT 7:40 SHARP EVERY MORNING NOW?

The Filth

22 PAGES

10. man made god

MAX... I REALLY DON'T THINK YOU *ARE* ALL RIGHT.

WE WERE MAKING REALLY GOOD *PROGRESS* LAST TIME...

HAVE YOU BEEN USING *DRUGS* AGAIN, MAX?

PLEASE, MAX, *SAY* SOMETHING... I KNOW IT'S IRENE'S *BIRTHDAY* BUT THAT'S NOT AN EXCUSE TO *START* ALL THIS AGAIN...

DOES *LARRY* KNOW ANYTHING ABOUT THIS?

MAX... PLEASE STAY HOME TODAY.

YOU'RE NOT WELL, MAX...

I SHOULD EXPLAIN TO HER HOW I'VE FINALLY CONQUERED MY HYPOCHONDRIA, MY CHRONIC AGORAPHOBIA, AND MY FEAR OF MALE PATTERN BALDNESS...

INSTEAD I STAY *SILENT* AND I STAY STRONG, AS THE WAY OF *BUDDHISMO* DICTATES.

STAY HOME.

I SHOULD TELL SHARON SHE'S SO *WRONG* ABOUT ME.

I KNOW EVERYBODY ONLY WANTS TO *HELP* ME...

MY MOTHER'S NAME WAS *IRENE SHATT*; SHE WOULD HAVE BEEN *83* YEARS OLD TODAY, SO THIS IS QUITE AN IMPORTANT DATE FOR ME.

WE ONLY *ARGUED* THAT LAST TIME BECAUSE SHE WANTED *TWO* LOTTERY TICKETS AND I'D BOUGHT *ONE* FOR HER AND NOT FOR MYSELF, WHICH MEANT I'D *HALVED* OUR CHANCES OF WINNING...

IT'S SO *STUPID,* ISN'T IT? WHEN YOU THINK ABOUT IT.

ALL THE STUPID REASONS PEOPLE FIND TO HATE ONE ANOTHER ON THE ROCKET RIDE TO THE *GRAVE.*

I WAS *STILL* ANGRY AT HER WHEN I CAME *HOME* FROM MY JOB AT THE STORE.

I COULDN'T WAIT TO TELL HER I'D HEARD GOD WAS ONLY A NEUROLOGICAL *SPASM*...AND THEN I FOUND HER JUST... *SITTING* THERE, LOOKING SO SMALL AND SO *DONE,* WITH THE *TV* ON.

SHH, RELAX...

I WAS IN SHOCK FOR ABOUT FOUR... OR MAYBE IT WAS *FIVE*... MINUTES BEFORE I NOTICED THE TICKET, FROZEN IN HER HAND.

WE'D JUST WON ABOUT *69* MILLION DOLLARS *MORE* THAN MY MOTHER'S HEART COULD HANDLE.

YOU CAN IMAGINE MY CONFLICTING EMOTIONS THAT DAY.

IN FACT...

YOU CAN PROBABLY EVEN *SEE* THEM.

HTT!

ANYWAY.

I KNEW I COULDN'T STOP BANK ROBBERIES WITHOUT BREAKING SOME LAW. THE CHANCES OF ME BEING THERE IN TIME TO HELP PREVENT ANY GIVEN *DISASTER* WERE REMOTE.

I NEEDED TO PROVE MYSELF AGAINST A DEFINING *VILLAIN,* IS WHAT I REALIZED.

SOME DARK ORWELLIAN NIGHTMARE CREW CREEPING UP FROM THE SEWERS AND THE CELLARS TO OPERATE ON HUMANITY.

AN ORGANIZED GANG OF AUTHORITARIAN MONSTERS.

AN ENEMY KNOWN AS "THE HAND"!

OH SHIT!

MOVE!

HERE THEY COME.

AN UNMISTAKABLE 21ST CENTURY THREAT MADE FOR ME; NOT JUST ORGANIZED CRIMINALS BUT WELL-DESIGNED *COMIC BOOK VILLAINS.*

POWER
BOOST

ENGAGE
FORKLIFT

IT'S ALL HAPPENING SO *FAST*...NOW...NOW I'M *OUTSIDE.*

I'M OUTSIDE AND EVERYONE CAN *SEE* ME.

GREG? NOT YOU...

CAN'T YOU SEE THEY'VE *BRAINWASHED* YOU I TURNED *YOU* INTO ONE OF *THEM*...

DON'T WORRY, GREG, IT'S ALL OVER... I'M *BROADCASTING* THIS WHOLE THING TO THE WORLD. EVERYONE'S WATCHING MY DEBUT ADVENTURE...

IT'S NOT AN *ADVENTURE;* YOU'VE BECOME A THREAT TO HEALTH.

A ROGUE GERM.

YOU AND YOUR COLLABORATORS DELIBERATELY INTRODUCED A CONTAMINATED PARA-PERSONA INTO SOCIETY; YOU CREATED *"SPARTACUS HUGHES"* WITH THE INTENT TO DESTABILIZE *STATUS Q* AND PROVOKE *THE HAND.*

AYE IN BY RA WEY, YIR CAMERAS ARE "BROADCASTEN" STRAIGHT OANTAY AN INTERNET *SNUFF SITE,* PAL.

THURRZ SICK BASTURTS WHAKKEN AFF RIGHT NOO, TRY- ENTAY TIME THURR CUM TAY YOOR LAST BREATH.

I WON'T WIND UP IN YOUR *SURGERIES!* I WON'T BE *LOBOTOMIZED* OR EXPERIMENTED ON...

I'M SORRY, MAX, BUT ACTUALLY YOU WILL.

YOU GOT WHAT YOU WANTED.

YOU SHOULD HAVE STAYED INDOORS WHERE YOU WERE SAFE.

DON'T DO THIS TO ME, GREG!

I'M THE HERO!

AND MY NAME'S NED SLADE.

YIR *CELLPHONE'S* RINGEN, BIG MAN.

WHAT?

HELL...HELLO?

MAX, THIS IS REGIS PHILBIN! MAX, YOU'RE ON *WHO WANTS TO BE A MILLIONAIRE...*

WHUH?

THE NEXT VOICE YOU HEAR WILL BE LARRY DE SANTO...

MAX, IT'S LARRY! CAN YOU BELIEVE IT... THIS IS FOR THE MILLION DOLLARS AND I SAVED YOU AS MY LIFELINE TILL NOW. LISTEN CAREFULLY...

I KNOW I CAN COUNT ON YOUR BRILLIANCE, BUDDY. WHAT IS THE GREEK WORD MEANING "HIDDEN"?

URRR

MAX?

PLEASE, SPEAK UP, I CAN'T HEAR YOU.

MAX? I ONLY HAVE FIFTEEN SECONDS. FOR CRYING OUT LOUD, I NEED YOU NOW...

The Filth

011
A VERY ENGLISH
NERVOUS BREAKDOWN

HE'S BACK.

HE'S *AT* IT AGAIN.

AND HE'S GOT A *WOMAN* WITH HIM NOW; IT'S LIKE MYRA HINDLEY AND IAN BRADY.

IT CAN'T BE *NORMAL.*

HE'S TAKING OUT *BAGS* OF STUFF...

FOR CRYING OUT LOUD, THE POLICE HAVE BEEN AND GONE.

THEY DIDN'T FIND ANYTHING BUT DEAD CATS.

HE DIDN'T *DO* ANY-THING.

THIS WAS MY *PLACE*.

I COULD UNWIND HERE AND BE KIND.

THIS HOUSE WAS WHERE I COULD COME TO GET AWAY FROM THE *HORROR*. WHERE I COULD FORGET THE JOB...

THAT'S WHAT YOU ALL *TOLD* ME.

GREG'S JUST A SAFE HOUSE, YOU SAID. HE'S NOT REAL, HE'S JUST A COVER STORY...

MY LOVELY CAT'S GONE. THE POLICE DUG UP MY BACK GARDEN, I'VE LOST MY JOB. THE NEIGHBORS THINK I'M A PEDOPHILE...

I'VE GOT NOTHING TO *LOSE* NOW, DO I?

SO I'M JUST GOING TO STAY HERE.

AND WAIT FOR THEM TO COME AND *GET* ME AGAIN.

MAYBE I *AM* JUST A LOONY WITH A STOLEN FACE.

MAYBE YOU'RE ALL RIGHT AND GREG IS JUST AN ARTIFICIAL PERSONALITY THEY INJECT INTO YOUR HEAD AND THERE YOU ARE.

MAYBE THERE IS NO GREG FEELY.

DMITRI *DEAD?*

THIS WASN'T SUPPOSED TO *HAPPEN;* YOU WERE SUPPOSED TO BE IN *CHARGE* OF GREG FEELY'S RECRUITMENT.

WHAT WENT WRONG, OFFICER NIL?

MIAMI?

THE CAT WENT WRONG, *CHIEF CONSTABLE MANDRILL.* ALL HE CARED ABOUT WAS THE FUCKING CAT.

WE DID IT *TWICE* AND I FELT SICK EACH TIME.

FEELY IS TOO FAR GONE.

HE'S NOT SELF. HE'S A NATURAL BORN *ANTI-PERSON.* I TRIED TO WARN YOU.

THE ORGANIZA-TION WAS MAKING A *BIG* MISTAKE TRYING TO *RECRUIT* HIM TO THE HAND INSTEAD OF JUST *KILLING* HIM.

NOW HE'S... *POLLUTED* US.

ARE YOU QUESTIONING *MOTHER DIRT'S* SUPERIOR AUTHORITY IN ALL MATTERS OF SUPERCLEANSING?

FEELY'S INDUCTION WAS *HER* IDEA, NIL.

SLADE.

ZIS YOO HUNTIN DOON THE METHA-DONE NOO?

THE POLIS URR WAITEN OOTSIDE.

MOAN, DON'T TELLIZ YIV TURNED INTAY A FUKKEN THIEVIN JUNKIE BASTURT IZ WELL?

PLEASE LISTEN TO WHAT CAMERON IS SAYING.

NED, PLEASE... YOU'RE ONLY GOING TO START HURTING PEOPLE IF YOU CARRY ON LIKE THIS.

GREG'S LOAST EEZ FUKKEN HEED; EEZ IN A LOATY TROUBLE...

A FEW MARE DAYS AN EEDUV MACHINE-GUNNED EEZ LOCAL PRIMURY SCHOOL.

C'MOAN BIG MAN. WINEETY GIT YOO CLEEND... CLEEND UP...

IT'S OUR NAMES, OFFICER SLADE, N. AND OFFICER SPECTOR, C.

IT'S YOU AND ME...WHENEVER THEY NEED A NEW NED SLADE, HE'S RIGHT HERE.

WE'RE ALL HERE.

PARAPERSONAS.

ALL OF YOU.

DON'T YOU *GET* IT?

THERE ARE PLACES LIKE THIS ALL OVER; THE HAND CAN TURN *ANYONE* INTO AN OFFICER, ANY TIME IT *HAS* TO.

BUT I'M NOT *HAVING* IT AND I'M NOT STOPPING NOW.

YOU CAN HELP ME OUT IF YOU WANT.

THEY PICKED ON THE WRONG MAN THIS TIME.

DEATH TO STATUS: Q.

ヨilth

22 PAGES

#12   SCHIZOTYPE

The
ヨilth

22 PAGES

#12   SCHIZOTYPE

The
ヨilth

22 PAGES

#12

SCHIZOTYPE

The
ヨilth

22 PAGES

#12   SCHIZOTYPE

The
ヨilt

The
Filth

#12 SCHIZOTYPE

The
Filth

12 SCHIZOTYPE

The
ヨilth

12 SCHIZOTYPE

Granted, my position as Executive Officer in the Accounts division of the Regional Developments Grants office was far from the glamorous James Bond style experience I first imagined... but it kept me running in the human race.

I didn't expect to be made redundant like that.

On top of which, they're coming to have me sectioned now.

I tried to explain about The Hand but all I got were blank stares and frantic scribbles in Department-issue notebooks.

They've got psychiatrists to say I'm the type who turns delusional and violent at the drop of a hat and I have to admit that, following the incident with the firearm at the chemists, they might be right.

They say I killed Tony with neglect and came up with The Hand as an excuse for being an alcoholic pervert deep inside. I couldn't stand it if that were true... I'd be so ashamed of myself...

YOU DON'T EVEN SEEM REAL NOW.

¿FFF?

OWWCH.

HEY. WHERE'S MY BEST PAL?

I WON'T BE LONG NOW, TONY.

The Filth

ISSUE #13
THEM vs US

22 PAGES

YOU WOULDN'T WANT TO *KNOW* WHAT YOU WERE.

OUT OF MY WAY.

YOU, THUNDERSTONE, BEMMER... THE WHOLE CRAZY GANG OF SOCIAL ACTIVISTS...

YOU WERE ALL GONNA DESTROY THE FOUNDATION STONE OF THE WORLD.

THE SYSTEM IS *PERFECT*, NED. IT *HAS* TO BE PERFECT; IT'S ALL THERE *IS*.

ATTACKING THE HAND IS LIKE FIGHTING YOUR OWN *IMMUNE SYSTEM*.

I DON'T FANCY YOU, MIAMI.

I WANT TO TALK TO WHO'S IN CHARGE!

Caution:

YOU CAN HAVE SOME *FRESH*, IF YOU LIKE.

MY MATE'S *AUNTIE*. RUNS THE SHOP, SEE?

THEY'D *LIKE* THAT.

I'M MEETING SOMEBODY SPECIAL, YOU SEE, AND THEY'RE DRAWN TO FLOWERS.

THE LITTLE ONES, I MEAN.

OH, RIGHT.

YOU'RE NOT THAT PEDOPHILE, ARE YOU?

311

NOW I DON'T WANT YOU TO BE UPSET WHEN YOU *SEE* HIM...BUT THERE'S A *STORY* TO IT.

SMOKE?

NOT FOR ME, THANKS.

I'M ALWAYS FRIGHTENED I'D END UP ADDICTED.

ONCE ON THE TRAIN TRACKS, JUST UP THE ROAD, SEE...WE FOUND A FUCKING *MONKEY PAW*, LIKE IN THE STORY, ONLY GIVING YOU THE *FINGER*.

AND NOT FAR AWAY, THERE'S THIS SCRAP OFF A FUCKED-UP OLD LEATHER JACKET WITH...GUESS WHAT'S IN THE POCKET?

...THE BIGGEST, SMELLIEST FUCKING *ROLL-UP* YOU EVER SAW.

I PRACTICALLY BEGGED THE STUPID BASTARD *NOT* TO SMOKE IT; BAD LUCK, I SAID. IT'S *OBVIOUS.*

"YOU ONLY WANT IT FOR YOURSELF," HE SAID.

SO HE TAKES A BIG FUCKING *DRAW*...AND BY THE TIME WE REACHED THE ALL-NIGHT GARAGE I COULD HEAR HIM SHOUTING, "I'M ORBITING THE FUCKING EARTH WITH A HOSEPIPE UP MY ARSE!"

HE COULDN'T *WAIT* TO TELL HIS AUNTIE.

HE WAS SO FUCKING FATALLY STONED, HE CLIMBED INTO THE RUBBISH COMPACTOR ON A CLEANSING LORRY. THOUGHT IT WAS A *STRETCH LIMO.*

"HOME, *JEEVES*..." WAS THE LAST THING I HEARD HIM SAY BEFORE THE GRINDERS CAME DOWN.

AND *I* WAS SO STONED I JUST STOOD THERE LAUGHING MY FUCKING HEAD OFF.

BERNARD.

"SPONGIE," WE USED TO CALL HIM.

SEEMS ONLY FAIR NOW.

I FIX HIS *DRIPS,* AND READ HIM A FEW COMICS. GIVES HIS AUNTIE TIME TO GET HER HAIR DONE AND HER TAROT CARDS READ.

AND HIM A DISCREET PUFF.

BLIND IN THE NOSE, SHE IS. NEVER SMELLS THE EVIDENCE.

USED TO BE A RIGHT *LAUGH,* HE WAS.

GO ON.

TELL HIM ABOUT THE *I-LIFE,* WHILE I'M HAVING A SHITE AND A READ.

I CAN'T TEMPT YOU *BACK*, SLADE?

WE RELOCATED THE *HAND*, IT'S A WHOLE NEW WORLD...AND THE SPECIAL SQUAD'S GONNA NEED YOU MORE THAN EVER.

NO MATTER *HOW* MANY PAINFUL AND GUILT-LADEN BLOW JOBS I PROMISE YOU?

YOU KNOW ME, MIAMI...

I ALWAYS PREFERRED UNDERCOVER WORK.

SUDSY-VORBA
FOR TWINGILL PARENT FARM

Micro-Sepsis

ANTIGEN MASKED FOR LETHAL
CLEANSING--GET SOME
FIST OFFICERS
DOWN HERE

MACRO-
DUMPERS
MOBILIZE TO
HOT ZONE--
WOUND DEBRIS
CLEAN-UP
UNDER WAY

This early teaser text for the series first appeared on Morrison's now-dormant website www.crackcomicks.com.

WHAT IS THE FILTH?

"Visit the centre of the earth

There you will find the global fire

Rectify it of all dirt

Drive it out with love and ire..."

sang Benedictus Figula

"The filth is Gerry Anderson for paranoid schizophrenics; a fluorescent Day-Glo trip through an abyss of internet porn, 'ironic' humor and disease pathology," roars writer Morrison, dispatching three massive warriors of the Uruk-Hai with a single razor-edged arc of his legendary Elven blade, Durinduryll, the Sword That Never Shuts Up. *"It's bigger, wilder, uglier and more heart-rending than the best summer blockbuster movie and if, like me, you love the awful smells of failure, shame, male pattern baldness and seedy compromise, then you're sure to revel in the squirming twists and turns of this exotic international spy-fi thriller, where games of identity,* madness and planetary hygiene combine with perverted sex, kitchen sink realism and ultra-technology to blind the mind's eye and infect the soul forever. Sights to scupper the sanity! Philosophies to burst the frontal lobes! People with combovers having sex! 'Certified UnCool Brutalist Pop-Fic EVERY MONTH for a twelvemonth and a day!'"

Yeah, right! And that's only the half of it. Grant Morrison's first creator-owned series since the groundbreaking cult hit THE INVISIBLES is a harrowing 13-issue rake through the middens of 21st century life, love, death and low self-esteem.

THE HAND STRIKES
THE HAND CARESSES
THE HAND INVOKES
THE HAND SIGNALS
THE HAND GIVES AND TAKES

WE ARE THE HAND THAT WIPES THE ARSE OF THE WORLD

PREPARE FOR INOCULATION.
STAY CLOSE TO THE SICK BAG.
THIS IS THE FILTH.

THE OOZE AND THE GOO

Wading into THE FILTH with Grant Morrison and Chris Weston

disease / Kobolds / underworld / reproduction / subterranean geology /
pressure / antibiotics / immune system / sperm sailing and the
cloacina etc. /

room – this one's been
turned off..

what are you doing, love?
I'm making the ultimate porno/

YOU BECOME
SHUNNED
UNTOUCHABLE.

• Klinshku in Amsterdam
He's in police station telli story.
gets cock out
Wow say cops.
'They're selling science in...'

bellamy/TV21/kubrd/
plutonian/purple/ultraviolet/
petrol blue/

crachl.comichs.com: a division of grantmorrison.com

Early notes by Morrison and augmented dolphin designs by Weston.

Hand propaganda posters.

THE PAPERVERSE

A creation of Hand Inkytech, the Paperverse is a so-called "concept-farm." Memetically-engineered for maximum imaginative crop yield, the Paperverse is an ongoing 2-dimensional narrative universe based on traditional American comic book fiction — these type of "super-hero" stories were found to be least resistant to real science considerations and therefore more fertile ground for development of imaginary technologies. Impossible machinery can be implanted within these permanently rolling "continuities," nourished into possibility and finally harvested into 3-D existence to enhance the ongoing operations of the hand.

Outlandish technologies and weapons are "written in" to the "story," tested by the "characters" in living scenarios maintained and farmed by experts. A large percentage of retrieved concepts are too frail to survive the return from the pressures of 2-D, of course, and disintegrate upon decompression into three dimensions, but this problem is now being attended to as the narrative development of "invulnerable" weapons and technology accelerates and yields spectacular durable results. Some fascinating and bizarre artifacts have already been recovered from the crushing fathoms of the Paperverse but this aspect of hand work has always been regarded as slightly frivolous and controversial by the higher echelons of the organization and remains so to this very day.

Secret Original concept sketches by Morrison.

THE STATUS QUORUM

The Status Quorum are fictional protectors of the Paperverse. Their journeys to other planets, dimensions and planes of existence are specifically designed for minimal scientific friction and maximum concept-crop yield.

The team at the beginning of THE FILTH #3 comprises:

ALPHA SAPIENS: Is Bill Tomney, a educationally-subnormal cleaner whose simple brain allows him to play host to the time-travelling micro-city of the Morlockoi. This minute, utopian society of tomorrow travels back in time to take over Bill's head. By enhancing his abilities and using the now-super-intelligent Alpha Sapiens as a messenger, the little visitors from the future go about the business of making human society better and more effective. Alpha Sapiens' primary mission is to arrange current events so that the world of today will eventually shrink and become the perfect, loving world of the majestic, miniaturized Morlockoi!!!

ULTRA-HUMANITARIAN: This Buddhist super-hero is an avatar of the Bodhisattva Avalokitesvara and has vowed to use his "siddhis" or super-powers to rid the earth of the so-called Four Sorrows of Existence — hunger, sickness, old age and death. So far, only hunger has partially succumbed to the might of Ultra-Humanitarian but his fight continues undaunted. His stare can shame a mountain range, his anger can turn the sun to water! Thank God he's on our side!

DARK STRANGER: This sinister lord of night and flies based his whole modus operandi on the life cycle of the swarming insects he found feasting on the corpses of his parents after returning from summer camp one year to find them dead — their bodies fought over by five separate serial killers, five undying maniacs Dark Stranger has vowed to destroy!

ZUR-VANN: One of mankind's oldest gods, Zur-Vann has returned from a 6,000-year-long mercy mission into space, only to find his mighty race long destroyed. Sole survivor of a tribe of ancient man-gods who once tamed the primal Earth, Zur-Vann now fights against the forces of chaos which threaten everyday life in Omnitropolis!

WOMANITE: Womanite is a new element: a soft mineral substance, created in his lab by Professor Mervin Coyle. A lonely bespectacled loser, Coyle sought to create his own sexy, synthetic companion but instead produced this ultra-militant feminist heroine. Womanite has only one weakness and that is Anti-Womanite — a living substance created to destroy her by the insane Professor Coyle, her enduring enemy. If Anti-Womanite ever touches Womanite the world will explode and possibly the universe as well.

MACHINE GIRL: Tess Bradlock was once a promising young gymnast until the horrific car crash, which left her father in a wheelchair and lovely Tess burned beyond all recognition and crippled from the ankles up. The distraught Doctor Bradlock invented and built the wind-up "machine girl" suit which allows Tess to move freely and "help people." Only dad can fix the suit which runs for five hours before needing "tinkering." Machine Girl's ponytail is made of living fiber optic filaments which respond to Tess' control and can be used either as a deadly weapon or as a handy computer interface!

The seventh member of the Status Quorum — and its first chairman — is SECRET ORIGINAL — now trapped in the three-dimensional world as the first living being to travel from fiction to reality. Crushed and folded into a wheelchair by the immense stresses of his passage from the 2-D world of the Paperverse, Secret Original is no longer an active member of the Status Quorum!

Designs for the Status Quorum by Weston.

HENRY V look...

NO. STOP SHOOTING.

STOP

specialist

constable

chief constable

Morrison's concept sketches for Ned Slade.

Preliminary and final character designs by Weston.

Sketches and character designs by Weston for Dmitri-9.

A Dmitri-9 maquette sculpted by FILTH fan Eric Tengren.

C. Weston

MOOG MERCURY
FREQUENCY PRIEST.

SEE NO EVIL
HEAR NO EVIL ?
SAY NO EVIL .

TALKS IN "RADIO" SPEACH!

"VIBRATOR-LIKE" BIO-TEC TOOL BELT

SANDALS - NOT SHOES.

CRONENBERG TECH:
POWER MAC³

YOU KNOW HOW EACH
NEW APPLE-MAC MODEL
LOOKS MORE AND MORE
ORGANIC? LET'S
EXTRAPOLATE THAT.

Weston designs for Miami Nil and Moog Mercury.

Ant children and iLife sketches by Weston.

THE CRAB

Designed for supercompression into the Paperverse, Crab One is the only one of the Hand wonder machines able to convert its structure from three dimensions to two and protect its crew from the distorting pressures of this incredible trip.

Crab One is captained by fraulein Harlotte Church, the only Hand agent to have attained distinction in all five divisions of the organisation.

Her crew is comprised of five lucky "virgins," each hand-picked from insane asylums and brothels around the world. When the band begins to play, when it's time to dive into the grinding, infinitely flattened jet-blue depths of the Paperverse, the girls take up their stations and sing their songs of loss and love and cynical scorn.

Crab One artwork by Weston.

Preliminary text description and Crab One crew designs by Morrison.

Captain Harlotte of the Crab One by Weston.

Crab One artwork by Weston.

A computer model of Crab One rendered by Gary Erskine.

THE DUMPTRUCK

The Hand Standard Series Dumptruck is a custom-built Cleansing vehicle brought to life by Hand Inkytech.

Each officer of the Hand is assigned a 2-seater personal Dumptruck.

The wheels of the Dumptruck are convertible into thrusters in aerial and submarine modes. Windows are fully evil-proofed and polaroid filtered. Engines run on refined 5-star ink and the Dumptruck can eat and digest five times its own weight in raw garbage in a 12-hour period.

The Dumptruck can accelerate to Ninth Gear — at these speeds space compacts and time begins to flow like a fast-moving beer, providing access to The Crack.

Weston's preliminary sketches and final designs for the Dumptruck.

"JAWS CLOSE"

TYRE "FLIPS" VERTICALLY.

Reference photos by Weston of a Dumptruck scale model sculpted by David Drage.

THE FILTH UNCENSORED!

Grant Morrison's complete script for the infamous "Pornomancer" chapter from THE FILTH #5, accompanied by unexpurgated artwork by Chris Weston.

Company: DC COMICS/Vertigo

Series: **the filth #5**

Title: **pornomancer** (22 pages)

Writer: Grant Morrison

Artist: Chris Weston

PAGE 1

Frame 1   Full page splash to open on. Go straight for the gut again, Chris — here's our protagonist, porn star Anders Klimaaks in action. He's dressed as the devil, with little horns and a forked clipped fake beard on his chin. He turns to look back over his shoulder at us with a grin (he always talks to camera, 'Alfie' style). Anders is in the midst of humping an actress dressed as an Amish girl with a ball gag in her mouth and her hands tied to the bedhead.

ANDERS: <u>HEY!</u>
ANDERS: COME ON IN!
ANDERS: DON'T BE SHY.

PAGE 2

Frame 1   Dozens of tiny close-up digital panels flickering across the entire page — fast cut shots of the sex film in superheated video-screen resolution. This mosaic of porn tiles is overlaid with a couple of horizontal frames.

BALLOON: UH
BALLOON: BITCH
BALLOON: AH
BALLOON: COCK
BALLOON: BABY
BALLOON: OHH
BALLOON: DEATH
BALLOON: HARDER
BALLOON: TRAMP

Frame 2   First of the horizontals shows a close up of a girl's hand with a cigarette between her fingers. Painted red nails.

ANDERS: WHO WOULD GIVE A FLOATING FUCK TO SEE THESE CRAZY MOVIES WHERE PEOPLE WITH STRICT RELIGIOUS PRINCIPLES GET TURNED INTO SHIT-WORSHIPPING PERVERTS BY THE DEVIL?

Frame 3   Pull back. The Amish girl, naked to the waist except for her untied, disarrayed bonnet. She takes a drag of her cigarette, bored. Anders in head and shoulders shot, foreground, is having his make-up touched up by a production girl. In background, a couple of guys are moving the lights and cameras. Anders shoots us his sidelong glance and wicked grin. He's always likeable and open.

ANDERS: ONLY THE STAUNCH FUNDAMENTALISTS OF THE WORLD.
ANDERS;   AND THAT IS LUCKY FOR <u>ME</u>.
ANDERS: TODAY IS '*ANAL QUAKERS*', SEQUELS TWO AND THREE.

Frame 4   Closer on Anders. Red face. Horns. Grin to camera.

ANDERS: <u>5 HOURS</u> FOR ME IN MAKE UP TO BECOME THE PRINCE OF DARKNESS AND FUCK SOME GIRL.
ANDERS: I FEEL LIKE I AM THE ELEPHANT MAN OF SEX.

PAGE 3

Frame 1   More tiny digital flickers.

BALLOON: UH
BALLOON: AH
BALLOON: HARDER
BALLOON: COCK
BALLOON: TRAMP
BALLOON: OHH
BALLOON: DEATH
BALLOON: BITCH
BALLOON: BABY

Frame 2   Horizontal insert. Close up on Anders fingers lighting a joint with a cigarette lighter.

ANDERS: THEN THERE IS REAL LIFE, WHERE BASICALLY I'M THE COMPLETE OPPOSITE OF THE JUDAEO-CHRISTIAN SATAN FIGURE; ANDERS KLIMAKKS IS A <u>HAPPY</u> KIND OF GUY WITH A WIDE RANGE OF INTERESTS.
ANDERS: BUT EACH PORNO ACTOR MUST HAVE HIS OWN SPECIALTY IF HE WANTS TO BE THE BIG STAR.

Frame 3   Anders holds the joint between his teeth and talks as he puffs some smoke. He makes an erect fist.

ANDERS: MAYBE IF THIS <u>ONE</u> GUY HAS THE KING OF COCKS, THEN THE <u>OTHER</u> GUY WHO IS NOT SO BIG MUST BE ABLE TO STAY HARD LIKE A POLICEMAN'S TRUNCHEON, YEAH?
ANDERS: THEN THERE IS THE <u>NEXT</u> GUY, WHO CAN MAKE THE GENETIC OINTMENT FLY ACROSS THE ROOM LIKE A SHELL FROM A HOWITZER.

Frame 4   As Frame 3 on the previous page. The girl tilts her head back against the wall and pouts a couple of smoke rings into the air. Her knees drawn up to her chest. Anders leans back, slumped and happy and blurred in his seat. He languidly points a video remote control at us.

ANDERS: EVERY STAR HAS THIS ONE SPECIAL THING NO OTHER HAS GOT.
ANDERS: BUT, I AM PROUD TO SAY, THERE IS ONLY THE ONE GUY IN THE ADULT BUSINESS WHO FIRES THE <u>BLACK</u> JUICE.

Frame 5   The digital flickers freeze and stop. As black ink jets across the camera and the face of the girl.

ANDERS: AND THAT GUY IS <u>ANDERS KLIMAKKS</u>.

PAGE 4

Frame 1   Cut to a police interview room in LA. Cop turning to look past us as he fills a plastic cup from the water dispenser. This is Detective Nick Welliwell. He's just used a remote to freeze the image on a small TV screen.

WELLIWELL: THEY FOUND YOU STROLLING BUCK <u>NAKED</u> DOWN THE MEDIAN STRIP ON HIGHWAY 101, ANDERS.

Frame 2   Close on water from the spigot filling the cup.

Frame 3   Welliwell walks towards us, carrying the cup. We see only his midsection.

WELLIWELL: YOU WERE CARRYING OVER <u>FIFTY</u> HARDCORE MAGAZINES, VIDEOS AND DVDs IN A TOMMY BAG.

Frame 4   Puts cup down beside some sex DVDs and videos on a table — all starring Anders Klimaaks. 'BEELZEBUGGER 2: THE SECOND COMING OF EVIL', 'DAD'S NAVY', 'ANAL QUAKERS', 'VIDEO CLIMAX 3', 'BUDDHIST BUTT BABES', 'SPUNK JIHAD'.

WELLIWELL: AND YOU HAVE NO <u>MEMORY</u> HOW YOU GOT TO BE THERE?

Frame 5   Anders Klimaaks. The sports bag on the table. He's carefully putting hardcore material back inside with one hand and picking up his water with the other. DVDs, videos, some magazines.

ANDERS: I TOLD YOU MY BRAIN HAS THIS MEDICAL FUCK-UP, MAN.
ANDERS: THESE ARE ALL THE MEMORIES I HAVE.

Frame 6   Anders Klimakks drinks some water. The porno is scattered on the table.

ANDERS: WHAT'S IN THIS <u>BAG</u> IS ANDERS KLIMAKKS.

PAGE 5

Frame 1   Cut to the roof of the police station. Welliwell stands at the edge looking over the city. He's having a smoke from a crack pipe. His partner John Whim joins him on the rooftop.

WHIM: SO AN AMNESIAC PORNO ACTOR FLASHES HIS DICK AT THE FAST LANE.
WHIM: IF I HAD <u>HIS</u> DICK, I'D BE TAKING OUT ADS IN THE <u>LA TIMES</u>.
WHIM: WHERE'S OUR CASE?
WELLIWELL: HE SHOOTS JET BLACK PEARLS, JOHN.
WELLIWELL: FOR CHRIST'S SAKE, THAT KIND OF THING ATTRACTS ATTENTION.

Frame 2   Welliwell is lifting a glass crack pipe to his lips, looking out thoughtfully. Whim appears behind him, a little concerned by his colleague's drug use but not wanting to say much.

WHIM: SO WE'RE HOLDING THIS GUY FOR FEDERAL?
WELLIWELL: *HUINN!*
WELLIWELL: THIS IS <u>WAY</u> BEYOND FEDERAL.
WELLIWELL: I EVER TELL YOU MY OLD MAN WAS A COP IN NEW YORK CITY?

Frame 3   Tight close. Detective closes his eyes and blows a cloud of smoke. He passes the pipe to the other guy who looks a little dubious and refuses.

WHIM: EVERY FUCKING DAY OF MY <u>LIFE</u>, NICK.
WHIM: YOU GOTTA LAY OFF THE CRACK PIPE.
WELLIWELL: WHO MADE <u>YOU</u> MY MOTHER?
WELLIWELL: GO ON. TRY SOME. YOU'LL FEEL GREAT.
WELLIWELL: I USED TO HEAR MY OLD MAN AND HIS CREEPY BUDDIES SOMETIMES, TELLING GHOST STORIES OR TALKING ABOUT ALL THE UNNATURAL SHIT THEY'D SEEN ON THE JOB.

Frame 4   Overhead shot. The detectives look over the parapet. Down in the car park, a Filth patrol vehicle pulls into the disabled space.

WELLIWELL: THERE WAS THIS ONE STORY ABOUT A CLEAN-UP CREW WHO COME UP FROM TUNNELS UNDER THE OLD PRECINCT HOUSE.
WELLIWELL: A SPECIAL SQUAD OF <u>UNTOUCHABLES</u> THEY MAKE DEAL WITH THE SHIT THE REGULAR GUYS WOULDN'T TOUCH.

Frame 5   Aerial shot of Los Angeles.

WELLIWELL: 'THE FILTH'... THAT'S WHAT THE OLD MAN AND HIS BUDDIES CALLED THEM.
WELLIWELL: CREEPY, HUH?
WELLIWELL: FUCKING CREEPY BUDDIES.

PAGE 6

Frame 1   Filth dumptruck in the car park.

Frame 2   People turn to look past us, reacting to the arrival of the Filth officer off-panel, whose POV we share.

Frame 3   Hand officer Jenesis Jones enters the station with absolute self-confident sexiness in her weird Hand uniform and Joan of Arc wig. All around her are little pull out panels showing close ups of her lips or her hand as it moves through space. Her boots on the floor. Her bum seen from behind. Build up a composite mosaic of her movement into the police station so that we're seeing it all at once. Jenesis Jones of the Filth has arrived. She's an officer of the Finger.

Frame 4   Desk cop.

Frame 5   Move in for a head and shoulder shot as Jones lifts her ID.

JONES: OFFICER JONES: <u>HAND</u> SUPERCLEANSING.
JONES: PRIORITY AUTHORISATION.
JONES: ANDERS KLIMAKKS, PLEASE.

PAGE 7

Frame 1   Zoom in on the ID. We can read the name JONES, JENESIS.

Frame 2   Jones is showing her ID to Anders Klimaaks in the interview room.

ANDERS: THERE IS NOTHING MORE I CAN SAY.
ANDERS: HOW ABOUT THE STORY OF <u>YOU</u>; YOU'RE A VERY SEXY LADY, THAT'S FROM WHERE I'M SITTING.

Frame 3   She reaches into her coat. Very business like.

JONES: WELL... I KNOW YOU CAME OUT OF <u>NOWHERE</u> FIVE YEARS AGO.
JONES: I KNOW YOU HAVE A NOVELTY PENIS WHICH DEFIES MEDICAL ANALYSIS.
JONES: OTHERWISE, <u>DON'T</u> TRY TO FUCK WITH ME, ANDERS; I HAVE <u>PMS</u>.

Frame 4   She lays her purse on the table.

JONES: SPERM SPECIMEN.
JONES: PLEASE.

Frame 5   Looking down over Anders Klimaaks' shoulders as he stands up and gets his cock out.

ANDERS: SURE.

Frame 6   Officer Jones' eyes widen as she stares at what we can't see.

ANDERS: THIS IS WHAT I DO FOR A LIVING.
JONES: JESUS!

PAGE 8/9

Frame 1   Anders Klimaaks' memories come to life. Tall vertical panel showing our hero in longshot, leaning against the brightly lit window of an Amsterdam sex shop. Neon and flesh and shiny covers. People pass like ghosts.

ANDERS: PORNO IS MY LIFE. IN THE WORLD OF ANDERS KLIMAKKS, IF THE GUY IS HARD AND THE GIRL COMES, THE PEOPLE WILL <u>PAY</u>.
ANDERS: HERE IS <u>AMSTERDAM</u> WHERE I MADE MY FIRST MOVIE.
ANDERS: 'MY LEFT-HAND COCK'.

Frame 2   These panels are a sequence of flowing images — panels which create a Z-shaped eye motion as we zoom and twist leading the reader across the page. First we see Jones looking at Anders as he comes across someone's head in a movie. We see only his top half.

JONES: FORGET FIVE YEARS AGO.
JONES: WHAT ARE YOU DOING IN <u>LOS ANGELES</u>, ANDERS?
ANDERS: I LIKE TO TRAVEL. I LIKE TO FUCK. I LIKE TO MAKE BIG BUCKS.
ANDERS: HARDCORE IS A GOOD BUSINESS FOR ME.

Frame 3   Far off longshot of a transatlantic passenger jet — KLM. Its trajectory on the page is such that it could easily have spurted from Anders' unseen cock in the previous image. The plane heads up to the top right of the page.

Frame 4   The plane comes towards us, slowly turning in the sky.

Frame 5   The plane comes closer, turning to pass us, heading towards the bottom right of the page.

ANDERS: I KNOW I FLEW FROM SCHIPHOL TO <u>LA</u> BECAUSE I HAVE THE TICKET STUBS.

Frame 6   Zoom into the window of the plane where Anders is looking out and down.

ANDERS: ALSO I HAVE THE <u>E-MAIL</u> THAT BROUGHT ME HERE SO I KNOW I WAS HIRED TO WORK ON THIS ONE MOVIE.

PAGE 9

Frame 1   Anders POV through the little plane window. Below, the flat circuit board sprawl of LA passes.

Frame 2   The plane is a tiny object seen in the sky above an observatory dome.

Frame 3   The dome is part of a stylish conversion in the Hollywood Hills. Now we see a long shot of Anders walking towards the front door.

ANDERS: WHAT WOULD <u>YOU</u> DO IF THE ORSON WELLES OF HARDCORE ASKED YOU TO PUT YOUR DICK IN HIS LATEST PRODUCTION?

Frame 4   Anders, seen in the fish-eye style of a door camera. He looks up.

ANDERS: OKAY, SO THIS GUY HAS A SCUMBAG REPUTATION WITH ALL THE GIRLS BUT FOR ME THIS WOULD BE BIG-TIME.

Frame 5   Head and shoulders of Anders. He turns to smile that charming, roguish smile once more and jerks his thumb as the front door opens. A silhouette appears — a man in a cowboy hat. We can see the camera mounted high on the doorframe for continuity with the previous panel.

ANDERS: HIS NAME IS TEX PORNEAU.

Frame 6   Tall vertical panel, the mirror of Frame 1. Close up on the heavily shadowed, mysterious face of the terrifying, outrageous spirit of unstoppable rapacious sexuality — TEX PORNEAU. His eyes glitter like cold blue ice in the shadows under the brim of his Stetson. He holds up a Panasonic DV.

PORNEAU: THE LATIN MOTTO ABOVE THE DOOR IS ALSO MY MEDITATIONAL MANTRA.
PORNEAU: IT READS *'FUCK... OR BE FUCKED'*.

PAGE 10

Frame 1   Jones takes off her coat, keeping her eye on us.

JONES: I'VE HEARD OF HIM.
JONES: IT'S NOT TEX PORNEAU WE'RE INTERESTED IN, ANDERS, IT'S YOU.
JONES: THIS SPECIALTY OF YOURS...

Frame 2   Anders is walking into Tex Porneau's mansion — Porneau himself walks about constantly naked and with a permanent hard-on which is hidden behind pixilations, the way they do on TV. He's a well-muscled man in his 50s, Germanic.

TEX: THEY TELL ME YOU HAVE THE BLACK JIZZ OF THE DEVIL IN YOUR BALLS, MISTER.
TEX: CARE TO PROVE IT?

Frame 3   Jones hangs her coat, glancing back at us. There's a slow-burning gradually building and thickening of the sexual tension.

JONES: TEX PORNEAU BOUGHT YOU A FLIGHT TICKET AND INVITED YOU TO APPEAR IN HIS LATEST PRODUCTION.
JONES: SOMETHING TASTY ENTITLED *'THE RAPE OF BEVERLEY HILLS'*, RIGHT?

Frame 4   The Jacuzzi seen from above. Porneau is showing the huge hot tub to Anders. A weirdly colored bubbling liquid is being pumped into the basin.

PORNEAU: PEOPLE SAY SIZE DOESN'T MATTER, ANDERS.
PORNEAU: YOU AND I KNOW DIFFERENT.
PORNEAU: SIZE IS EVERYTHING.

Frame 5   Anders smiles in close-up.

ANDERS: THAT WAS THE NAME OF THIS MOVIE; I DON'T KNOW WHICH GIRL WAS BEVERLEY HILLS.
ANDERS: I CAN'T REMEMBER...

Frame 6   The Jacuzzi is filled with writhing naked girls and Anders Klimaaks. The strangely-hued water boils and froths as the orgy gets underway.

ANDERS: IT'S TRULY FUCK OR BE FUCKED, MAN.

PAGE 11

Frame 1   We're looking at Anders in the flashing colored light. He's being pulled down in to a seething mass of flesh, arms wide. He looks ecstatic, drugged to the eyeballs.

ANDERS: THIS WATER IS LIKE TOO MUCH JELLY.
ANDERS: THIS IS NOT BUBBLES.
ANDERS: ARE THERE FISH HERE?

Frame 2   From behind Anders. His arms are wide. He's silhouetted by the light of the rising sun. The entire circular chamber inside the dome is blazing with intense light. People thrash and the water explodes and bubbles, gouting like lava. Things turn cubist.

Frame 3   Screaming terror, huge 'fish' forms thrash in the bubbling weirdly colored Jacuzzi froth. People sucked under into the maelstrom of slithering bodies, thrashing coiling tails. The light is intense. Wild screaming cubist chaos. Anders looks up at us, into the light, arms wide in supplication.

ANDERS: WHY IS EVERYONE SCREAMING?

Frame 4   Tex films the splattering horror. Lit from below. Frightened girls crouch by his chair, gazing in terror. In foreground, froth rises, clutching hands and screaming mouths as heads bob past in front of us, trying to escape from the Jacuzzi. Normal POV now, simple stark super-real image without the cubist distortions. Fierce light.

Frame 5   Cut to Anders in longshot, staggering naked along the highway. Sun overhead. Noon light. Cars flash by streaking into strobes and lines. Jones walks beside him.

ANDERS: LUCKY I MANAGED TO GET MYSELF AND MY BAG OF MEMORIES OUT OF THERE.

PAGE 12

Frame 1   Officer Jones leans across the table, engrossed, besotted. She leans her head on her arms which are crossed on the desk. Faint wisps of visible infra-red radiation rise from her as she heats up.

JONES: MY... ah... MY JOB IS TO IDENTIFY AND TARGET THINGS THAT DON'T BELONG IN THE WORLD.
JONES: I WANT TO KNOW WHY <u>TEX PORNEAU</u> NEEDS YOUR SEMEN.

Frame 2   Anders and Jones face one another across the table. Anders is beating off under there but we don't see anything, we just know what's going on. More infra-red.

ANDERS: FOR ME IT SEEMS LIKE… LIKE <u>EVERYBODY</u> WANTS MY SEMEN, MISS.
ANDERS: I SHOULD NOW MENTION THAT I'M JUST ABOUT READY TO EJACULATE.

Frame 3   Same POV. Jones climbs up onto the table, heading towards Anders Klimaaks as if magnetised by lust. She's picking up the purse. He's looking down, hand pumping under the table. His body is perfectly sculpted. He's struck this dramatic pose before.

JONES: HERE.

JONES: I'LL CATCH IT IN THIS.

Frame 4   Same POV. Jones crawls across the table. Fumes of radiant infra-red heat as the scene dissolves into heat distribution patterns.

JONES: YOU DO KNOW I FIND YOU <u>VERY</u> ATTRACTIVE, MR. KLIMAKKS.

Frame 5   Zoom in for a close-up. His left hand pulls her head forward. Their lips part to kiss. All is red and hot. In between the two faces is TV static.

ANDERS: ANDERS.

PAGE 13

Frame 1   The static fills a long thin horizontal panel across the top of the page.

Frame 2   Jones lies on her back, head tilted towards us, upside down. She lifts her arm to speak into her wrist radio. Her clothes have been pulled open, trousers around her ankles.

JONES: SHIT.
JONES: FUCK.

Frame 3   Move around to the side as she lifts her wrist radio to her lips.

JONES: <u>JONES TO CENTRAL!</u>
JONES: I'VE COMPLETELY BLOWN THIS ASSIGNMENT.
JONES: ANDERS KLIMAKKS OVERWHELMED ME WITH SOME KIND OF MAXI-PHEROMONE AND GOT <u>AWAY</u>.

Frame 4   Her free hand moves down to scoop between her legs.

JONES: I NEED TO CONFIRM <u>PERSON/ANTI-PERSON COMPLEX ALERT</u>. STATUS: V.

Frame 5   Close. She lifts her hand into shot and we see what looks like ink hanging in strings from her fingers.

JONES: REQUEST <u>IMMEDIATE</u> LETHAL CLEANSING BACK-UP.

PAGE 14

Frame 1 Establishing shot of Tex Porneau's observatory home. Skyline of the LA basin and the Hollywood hills. Beautiful orange sky of late afternoon. Dusty sunstruck haze of LA. The light blazing in the mirrored walls of downtown skyscrapers way off in the basin.

Frame 2 The cops at the ornate door of the observatory. It's the same place we saw earlier (page 9). They look at one another a little nervously. Detective Nick Welliwell takes another gulp of crack. Cameras everywhere.

WELLIWELL: BUSY ADDRESS.
WELLIWELL: THERE'S EVEN A <u>FED-EX</u> TRUCK, FOR CHRIST'S SAKES.
WHIM: DON'T YOU THINK YOU'RE STARTING TO ABUSE THAT STUFF?

Frame 3 Welliwell rings doorbell.

WELLIWELL: FUCK YOU.
WELLIWELL: IT'S RECREATIONAL. IT'S UNDER CONTROL.

Frame 4 From behind. The door opens and we're behind the naked Tex Porneau himself. The detectives look down at his unseen dick with shock. Blows smoke and drops the crack pipe.

WELLIWELL: TEX PORNEAU?
WELLIWELL: DETECTIVES WHIM AND WELLIWELL. <u>LAPD</u>. WE'RE HERE TO TALK TO YOU ABOUT ANDERS...
WELLIWELL: SHIT.

Frame 5 Powerful head and shoulders shot capturing the full Tex Porneau mystique. Huge cigar in his fingers. Eyes shadowed by his hat brim, glittering in the gloom. Germanic, stocky, monstrous. Behind him, figures creep forward from the depths of the house. Tex should have a few huge sleek Dobermans around too. Stealth fighter dogs.

TEX; NO TIME FOR TALK, HONEY.
TEX: YOU CAME TO MY DOOR. THAT MEANS *'FUCK OR BE FUCKED'*.

PAGE 15

Frame 1 The detectives look a little perplexed but try to stay tough and in charge of this situation. Reality is slowly falling away however. People come up behind the cops, stealthy perverts and hollow-eyed porno stars carrying hoods, harnesses, restraints, clothing, wigs, whatever. These are the Extras — the endless parade of weirdoes trapped in Tex's never-ending sex film.

WELLIWELL: YEAH. SURE THING, SCUMBAG.
WELLIWELL: WE'RE HERE TO ASK A FEW VERY SERIOUS AND...

Frame 2 The cops are suddenly overwhelmed. A rubber doll like face is being rolled down over Welliwell's forehead. He's going into real panic. The grinning, drugged and dressed-up Extras restrain his arms and legs, pinning him.

WELLIWELL: <u>AUU CHRIST!</u> JESUS CHRIST, <u>NO!</u>
WELLIWELL: WHAT <u>IS</u> THAT THING!
WELLIWELL: <u>WHAT'S THAT COMING DOWN THE HALL, JOHN!!</u>

Frame 3 The pervs pull a mask over Whim's head. His arms flail.

WELLIWELL: *GNNUMMF*
WHIM: NO... JESUS, NO YOU CAN'T DO THIS *TRRWMMF*

Frame 4 Max is behind Detective Whim, mounting him with a cold thin smile. We can only see Whim's boggling eyes through the holes in his insectile bondage mask. His zipped mouth gives away nothing of the intense feelings Whim is experiencing.

WHIM: <u>NAUUUU</u>
TEX: JUST <u>RELAX</u>. YOU'RE VERY BEAUTIFUL WHEN YOU LET GO. VERY SEXY, BABY.

Frame 5 Tex leering.

TEX: THAT'S GOOD, YEAH. YOU CAN TAKE IT.
WHIM: <u>MMWHHAAUU</u> (From off)

PAGE 16

Frame 1 Rolling from foreground, a monstrous dungball of garbage — cans and bin bags and newspapers and old curries — that's rolled around the house by slaves in gimp gear. They crawl across the ball, moving it the way dung beetles herd their shit globe across the desert, rolling it here and there. This huge ball stopped for a moment. The struggling fetishized detectives are being pulled towards the horrible giant ball. Welliwell is shrieking. Whim is broken, limp.

WELLIWELL: MMMUUIIIIII
TEX: GOOD GIRLS.
TEX: NOW GO, JOIN IN, AND DON'T <u>BOTHER</u> ME.
TEX: I'M CREATING PORNOGRAPHIC HISTORY.

Frame 2 The scarab-people help Whim up onto the ball of garbage where he can only cling there like one of them. Tex looks down and point off panel, showing the struggling Welliwell something awful which is coming in from off panel.

TEX: A NEW WORLD DEMANDS A NEW KIND OF <u>HARDCORE</u>. YOU'LL ALL LEARN THAT SOON ENOUGH.
TEX: I WANT YOU ALL TO MEET ONE OF THE STARS OF MY <u>ULTIMATE</u> MOVIE.

Frame 3 A huge, magnified sperm glides like a shark between the girls' legs towards Tex. It propels itself through the air with a long tail.

TEX: DON'T WORRY.
TEX: THIS ONE'S <u>DORMANT</u>. NEUTERED.

Frame 4 Tex Porneau crouches down to pet the eerie giant spermatozoon. A mad light in his eye.

TEX: UNLIKE ITS MANY, MANY GREEDY BROTHERS.

PAGE 17

Frame 1 Big background shot of the mansion interior cut into tall verticals to register the movement as the ball rolls away grotesquely with Detectives Whim and Welliwell now indistinguishable form the crawling, faceless scarab people. Four insect figures now scramble purposefully across the ball, piloting it off down the corridor into the interior of the mansion.

TEX: THE EXISTENTIALISTS <u>FALTERED</u> ON THE BRINK OF THE GAPING <u>VOID</u>.

Frame 2 The creeping crawling people roll the garbage ball away.

TEX; 'NAUSEA'... THAT'S WHAT THOSE LIMP-DICK INTELLECTUALS FELT.
TEX: THEY WERE <u>AFRAID</u> OF THE BIG BLACK PIT. SCARED OF LOSING THEIR WEENY-WEENY DICKLETS IN THE ASSHOLE OF BEING!

Frame 3 Around the corner.

TEX: <u>NOT ME! BY GOD, NOT TEX!</u>
TEX: <u>I'M GONNA FUCK THE ABYSS RAW!</u>
TEX: <u>I'M GONNA MAKE IT HOLLER LIKE LOLITA!</u>

Frame 4 Tex turns round and grabs a poor guy in a FedEx outfit. Tex has his DV camera in one hand, always ready.

FEDEX: LISTEN, MISTER... THIS IS SOME PLACE YOU GOT HERE BUT I... I THINK THERE'S BEEN A <u>MISTAKE</u>.

PAGE 18

Frame 1 We follow Tex towards a viewing window up a spiral stair. He's dragging the Fed-Ex guy behind him and his creeping capering posse of Extras follow. Crying women in corners.

FEDEX: PLEASE, WHAT ARE YOU DOING?... IN THE NAME OF CHRIST, I'M JUST THE DELIVERY GUY.
FEDEX: YOU CAN'T FUCKING DO THIS...
TEX: DON'T GIVE ME THIS UNPROFESSIONAL BULLSHIT, HONEY.
TEX: I GET A THOUSAND GIRLS THROUGH HERE WHO MANAGE TO DO WHAT THEY'RE TOLD <u>WITHOUT</u> BLEATING LIKE LOSERS.

Frame 2 Fed-Ex tries to protest but he's having a weird feathered crest strapped under his chin by Tex's relentless entourage of Extras.

FEDEX: PLEASE... I HAVE TWO YOUNG BOYS!

Frame 3 Cardboard beak arrangement on elastic is pulled over the Fed-Ex guy's face. Tex takes up position behind him, hand on his shoulder, cooing menacingly in the hapless man's ear.

FEDEX: I ONLY CAME TO MAKE A DELIVERY
TEX: YOU'LL GET YOUR DELIVERY, PRINCESS.
TEX: TEX PORNEAU STYLE.

Frame 4 Tex is filming over the guys shoulder as he penetrates him from behind. We're close up, so we don't see anything other than the reactions. Bug eyed Fed-Ex guy, grinning icy Tex as he films his masterpiece.

FEDEX: **WAAUUH GODDD!**
TEX: YOU <u>LIKE</u> THAT, HUH? JUST A SHY LITTLE ENGLISH <u>SCHOOLGIRL</u>, AREN'T YOU?
TEX: YOU WANT TO SEE DADDY FUCK <u>LOS ANGELES</u> HUH?
TEX: <u>DADDY CHAOS?</u>
TEX: **DADDY DEATH?**

(Tex's yells get bigger, more orgasmic)

Frame 5 Tall vertical. The observatory. The centre of the dome is pulled back and the observatory shoots light in to the air.

TEX: **DADDY MADNESS!**

(Letters get huge in a ridiculous crescendo)

PAGE 19

Frame 1   Giant sperm leap from the bubbling boiling Jacuzzi hurtling skyward towards the open dome.

Frame 2   Tex throws the shocked, traumatized FedEx guy aside. Marches forward with his erect penis hidden behind pixel fuzz.

TEX: THESE NEW KIDS... WITH THEIR SLEAZECORE HEROIN VOMIT PORN... THESE DROOPY PUNKS THINK <u>THEY</u> CAN STEAL THE HARDCORE CROWN FROM TEX PORNEAU.
TEX: FORGET IT.

Frame 3   Tex's cowboy boots in foreground ground level as he walks out of shot. In background the pervs descend upon the Fed-Ex guy and drag his flailing body away.

TEX: TRIPLE <u>IMAX</u> 3-D SUPER-EXTREME HARDCORE.
TEX: THE ULTIMATE EQUATION...

Frame 4   Overhead shot as Tex walks out onto the circular deck around the dome. There are cameras on tripods, pointing at Beverley Hills.

TEX: <u>SEX = DEATH = BUCKS!</u>
TEX: I AM THE FUTURE!

Frame 5   Tex Porneau mans the cameras profile from waist up, angling the camera down as he fucks a girl up the ass. His arm around her waist, she's bent over the balcony rail, eyes wide with alarm and shock as he calmly glides in.

TEX: ARE YOU READY FOR THE MONEY SHOT, MISS HILLS?
TEX: <u>SCENE ONE!</u>
TEX: <u>TAKE 1!</u>

PAGE 20

Frame 1   Horizontal shot. Filth patrol vehicle racing towards us with streaming speedlines of streets around.

DMITIRI: I THOUGHT YOU SAY YOU <u>REMEMBERED</u> HOW TO DRIVE, SHIT-FOR-HEAD?

Frame 2   Close in on the driver and passenger. The driver is Dmitri 9. The chimpanzee assassin. The passenger Ned Slade. Slade looks at some pornos, Dmitri is intense, smoking a big joint.

DMITIR;   <u>HOOUUP</u>
DMITIR: HAVE A NICE DAY! HAVE A NICE DAY!
DMITIRI: <u>LET THEM SPEND ONE DAY IN A FREEZING COLD SPACESUIT FULL OF SHIT!</u>
SLADE: CHIMP-LANGUAGE FOR *'WE'RE DEPLOYING DUMPTRUCKS TO SECURE THE CLEAN-UP ZONE'.*
SLADE: GOT THAT?
SLADE: THIS IS <u>SLADE</u>: I'M TRYING MY BEST TO FIT IN.

Frame 3   Three vertical panels. Longshot of Jones running across the street. Evening shades now on the clean streets of Beverly Hills' rich shopping pavilions.

RADIO: ANDERS KLIMAKKZZ////ACTIVITY IN ZONE MAY HEAT UP AROUND////STATUS: W ALERT
RADIO: ///ORDERS FROM///
JONES: WHAT ?
JONES: I CAN'T HEAR.

Frame 4   She comes closer. Yells into her wrist radio.

JONES: THERE'S THIS... <u>CRACKLING</u> NOISE FROM EVERYWHERE. THE HILLS... THIS SMELL...
JONES: IT'S LIKE FIRECRACKERS AND AMMONIA OR...

Frame 5   Closer. She reacts as she sees Anders off panel.

JONES: I <u>GOT</u> HIM!
JONES: HE'S ON <u>RODEO DRIVE!</u>

PAGE 21

Frame 1   Horizontal. Anders turns, he's with a gorgeous looking, impeccably dressed woman. We're looking over Jones' shoulders as she aims her hypo gun at Anders.

JONES: <u>ANDERS KLIMAKKS!</u>
ANDERS: HAVE WE MET?
ANDERS: DO YOU WANT ME TO SIGN YOUR PANTIES?

Frame 2   Move in on Anders. The face of genuine innocence, he shows off his new suit proudly. The glamorous woman hangs on his arm and offers a challenging look.

ANDERS: THIS BEAUTIFUL HORNY LADY WAS BUYING ME A TERRIFIC <u>SUIT</u>, YOU SEE...
WOMAN;   PLEASE... YOU <u>CANNOT</u> KILL THIS MAN.
WOMAN: DO YOU REALISE HE HAS A TEN INCH PENIS?

Frame 3   Looking up, past Jones' head as she lifts it, sensing something from above. We can see up past the storefronts to the sky where a weird swarm can be seen, turning like swallows in flight and angling sharply downwards.

JONES: OH, YES I DO.
JONES: STAND AWAY!
JONES: ANDERS KLIMAKKS: YOU HAVE BEEN IDENTIFIED AS A POTENTIALLY LETHAL ANTI-PERSON!

Frame 4   Anders looks up. A faint frown of recognition.

ANDERS: AH.
ANDERS: MAYBE <u>THIS</u> IS WHY MY SPUNK HAS BEEN GROWN TO GIANT SIZE AND USED AS A WEAPON.

Frame 5   Overhead shot. Jones looks up can't believe what she's seeing. We have vague hints of shapes diving down towards her. Shadows on the ground.

JONES: NO
JONES: FUCKING
JONES: WAY.

JONES: **HAND ASSIST!**

PAGE 22

Frame 1   Then BANG shock end splash as the sperm of Anders Klimaaks explode through Jones and the woman with her shopping bags. In background, the fastest of the monster cells are bursting through the womb of any woman they can find. It's the giant size sperm invasion of Beverly Hills.

the filth created by Morrison and Weston
grant morrison writer
chris weston penciller
gary erskine inker
hifi color & seps
clem robins lettering
carlos segura cover artist
steve bunche associate editing
karen berger editor
more filth at crackcomicks.com & vertigocomics.com

Promotional art for the series drawn by Weston, colored by
Matt Hollingsworth, and featured in Diamond's *Previews* catalog.

BIOGRAPHIES

Grant Morrison has been working with DC Comics for more than twenty years, beginning with his legendary runs on the revolutionary titles ANIMAL MAN and DOOM PATROL. Since then he has written numerous bestsellers — including JLA, BATMAN and *New X-Men* — as well as the critically acclaimed creator-owned series THE INVISIBLES, SEAGUY, THE FILTH, WE3 and JOE THE BARBARIAN. Morrison has also expanded the borders of the DC Universe in the award-winning pages of SEVEN SOLDIERS, ALL-STAR SUPERMAN, FINAL CRISIS, BATMAN, INC. and ACTION COMICS.

In his secret identity, Morrison is a "counterculture" spokesperson, a musician, an award-winning playwright and a chaos magician. He is also the author of the *New York Times* bestseller *Supergods*, a groundbreaking psycho-historic mapping of the superhero as a cultural organism. He divides his time between his homes in Los Angeles and Scotland.

Chris Weston is a British illustrator who has enjoyed a long career working for the comic-strip industries on both sides of the Atlantic. After getting his start drawing Judge Dredd for the weekly UK magazine *2000 AD*, Weston has gone on to contribute art to BATMAN, SUPERMAN, *The Fantastic Four*, SWAMP THING, and THE INVISIBLES for DC and Marvel. However, he is probably best known for his work on two creator-owned series: THE FILTH (with writer Grant Morrison) and *Ministry of Space* (with writer Warren Ellis). His more recent comics work includes the J. Michael Stracyzynski-written and Eisner Award-nominated Marvel series *The Twelve*, for which he also wrote a prequel story entitled *The Twelve: Spearhead* that won an AICN Comics Award for Best One-Shot. Since then he has branched out into the world of film concept art and storyboards, working with director Albert Hughes on movie projects like *The Book of Eli* and a live action adaptation of Katsuhiro Otomo's *Akira*. Most recently, Weston has enjoyed a popular and growing sideline in producing limited edition silkscreen prints based on popular films.

Gary Erskine began his comics career drawing for Marvel UK and the British anthology magazines *2000 AD* and *Crisis*. In 1993 he left Marvel UK to create the Tundra graphic novels *The Lords of Misrule* with writers Dan Abnett and John Tomlinson and *Pale Horse* (later published by Dark Horse as *Hypersonic*) with writers Steve White and Dan Abnett. A third, unfinished Tundra project — *City of Silence* with writer Warren Ellis — was reborn in 2000 as an acclaimed Image miniseries.

In 2002 Erskine was approached by artist Chris Weston to ink Grant Morrison's groundbreaking Vertigo maxiseries THE FILTH, and his Vertigo work continued in the titles ARMY@LOVE with writer/artist Rick Veitch and GREATEST HITS with writer David Tischman and artist Glenn Fabry. Over the years he has also collaborated with Mark Millar, Garth Ennis, James Robinson, Kurt Busiek, Alex De Campi, and Brian Wood on a wide variety of features, including *Captain America*, *Judge Dredd*, *The Avengers*, *The Massive*, *Star Wars*, *Doctor Who*, *The Terminator*, and *Transformers*.

In addition to his comics work, Erskine teaches design workshops, provides storyboards and concept art to the video game, film, and television industries, and mentors film students at the Royal Conservatoire of Scotland. He is currently working on motion comics for Madefire as well as crafting the independent comics titles *Roller Grrrls*, *Incendiary.US*, and *Zachariah Gunn: Dakota*. He lives in Glasgow, Scotland with his wife Mhairi and their cats Meg and Mog, and he dislikes writing in the third person.

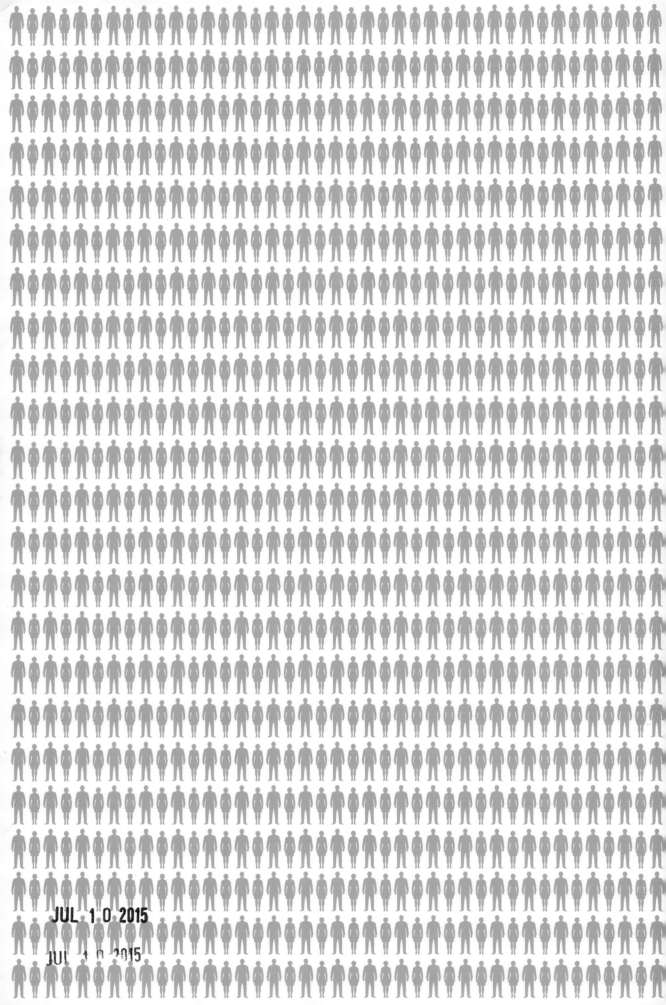